When the
Womb
is
Empty

When the
Womb
is
Empty

A Positive Approach to Infertility

Ray & Rebecca
Larson

WHEN THE WOMB IS EMPTY

Ray and Rebecca Larson

Copyright © 1988 by Ray and Rebecca Larson
Printed in the United States of America
ISBN: 0-88368-198-6

Editorial assistance for Whitaker House by Valeria Cindric.

The poems *Don't Let Me Forget, Lord* by Denise Majewski and *Psalm 139 For the Infertile Woman* by Gaye Ruschen first appeared in the August/September, 1985 issue of *Stepping Stones,* Box 11141, Wichita, Kansas 67211, and are used by permission.

Unless otherwise noted, Scripture quotations are taken from the *New International Version* of the Holy Bible, copyright © 1973, 1978, 1984, International Bible Society, and are used by permission. Quotations marked TLB are taken from *The Living Bible,* copyright © 1971 by Tyndale House Publishers, Wheaton, Illinois, and are used by permission. Quotations marked NASB are taken from the *New American Standard Bible,* copyright © The Lockman Foundation, 1960, 1962, 1963, 1968, 1971, 1972, 1973, 1975, 1977 and are used by permission.

Many of the names and addresses of adoption agencies are taken from the *Adoption Factbook* published by the National Committee for Adoption, 1930 17th Street, N.W., Washington, D.C. 20009 and are used by permission.

DEDICATION

To the many Christian couples who, in the midst of infertility, battle the hopelessness of ever raising a family. There are miracles ahead!

and

To Bethany Christian Services who are a bright light in a very dark time.

CONTENTS

CHAPTER ONE

No Birth-Days

"I'm sorry, Mr. Larson, but the test was absolutely negative," the nurse explained.

"Please check again, there must be some mistake," I retorted.

"No, there is no mistake, the findings are conclusive," she patiently stated once again.

As I hung up the phone, the reality hit me—like cold water interrupting a hot shower: The Larsons would never have children of their own. No little boys to take to ball games; no little girls who would look like their mommy.

How could God be so cruel? After all, Rebecca and I had both committed our lives in service to Jesus Christ and had agreed to get established in ministry before having children. Now after four years of waiting, our reward had been denied us.

Unwilling to admit defeat, I went in again to my doctor and demanded another fertility test. Our physician had tolerated my requests for testing over and over, but the results never changed. Unless God miraculously intervened, conceiving children of our own would be impossible.

There would be no *birth*-days in our family. No announcements of pregnancy, no baby showers, no delivery room.

The latter years of our lives would be spent all alone. The joy of being parents and grandparents would elude us.

Weeping together, Rebecca and I struggled with bitterness. It was difficult not to blame God. Almost everyone and everything has the ability to reproduce! Animals do; plants can; even amoebas divide. It is a normal part of being alive. Yet here we were, a rare exception to God's blessing, unable to fulfill one of the first great commandments in Genesis: "Be fruitful and multiply."

A Natural Reaction

This latest disaster appeared to be just another event in a long line of pain for both of us. I had grown up in foster homes; Rebecca had been mauled by a German shepherd dog as a young adult. The list went on. In spite of our past experiences, we had remained faithful, praising God despite our sufferings. But no children? Even the wicked raise kids! It seemed too much to handle.

No words of thanks or praise sounded from our lips this time. The "hallelujahs" and "glory to God's" were silenced by the roaring emotions of rejection, inadequacy, and failure. Our lives were shattered; our dreams dashed. The God whom we loved so much seemed strangely silent, leaving us in a state of bitterness and confusion.

We wonder now how we could have responded to God in such a manner, but at the time it was our most natural reaction. We knew we weren't going to reject God, but there was a definite pinch in our communication line to the Throne.

During our four years of married life, there were nights when Rebecca and I would awaken with a start to realize we had had the same nightmare at the same time on the same night. Smiling in relief to know it was not reality but only a bad dream, we would hug each other and return to peaceful sleep.

But this nightmare was real life. Rebecca and I hoped we would wake up and discover that the horrifying ordeal was over. But the harsh reality greeted us every morning and accompanied us throughout the day.

For days we existed in a spiritual stupor. A state of emotional comatose pervaded our whole life and affected our entire being. Every thought returned to the dreaded fact that this is not a one-night stand with a bad dream; this is for the rest of our lives.

Living in the Twilight Zone

In the midst of this trying time, Rebecca and I couldn't seem to feel anything. I added to the problem by not wanting to deal with the situation or discuss it with my wife. My defense was a code of silence—each person alone in their own fox hole.

It was a technique developed during my years spent in foster homes. When I accepted new life in Christ, I thought those old responses were put behind me. But, much to my surprise, they returned to me now as easily as riding a bike after years without practice.

My wife wanted to rise above our shock and allow God to heal our wounds. Without knowing it, however, I had already set my course: I believed that the problem would simply go away.

Ironically, it was easy for me to assume an apparent air of unconcern when talking to other people. But within my heart the pain lay latent, waiting to break through to my attention at any moment. In front of others, I acted as though I had total victory over the situation. Yet, I avoided the communication with my wife that would have opened the door for the Holy Spirit to begin the necessary healing.

The result was a spiritual "twilight zone" that fixed us somewhere between victory and defeat. Rebecca was forced to exist there with me because I refused to take a course of action. I was numb, just plain numb.

In bed, Rebecca and I would lie together like lifeless forms. We couldn't talk because all conversation eventually led back to the forbidden zone: infertility. For months I kept hoping that we would find it had been a mistake, a cruel joke, a bad dream.

The ever-present reality was unchanging, however. In the Larson home there would be no *birth*-days! No visiting Mommy and child doing well in the maternity ward. No birth-days! No kindergarten graduations and trips to Disneyland! No birthdays! No toys under the Christmas tree or Easter baskets to hide. Just an empty nest and a couple who profess faith in Jesus Christ yet struggle to survive.

In His faithfulness, however, God ultimately gained the victory. The results of our struggle prove distinctly that God was and is in charge of our lives. We learned that He can move mountains in order to fulfill His purpose for His children. What a compassionate, loving Father we have.

Ahead of Rebecca and I lay a long road that we had yet to walk in order to fully comprehend the course God had planned for our family. At this juncture, all I could view was the pain that emerged from a deep desire to raise children, to love a family, and to bring them up in God's presence and order. The dream of giving my children the childhood I had missed was now a pile of rubble.

I was so immersed in my own loss I failed to see that my wife, too, had precious hopes and dreams that had been dashed. In the next chapter Rebecca describes, in her own words, the grief that she as a woman experienced.

CHAPTER TWO

Why Me, God?

The dream I harbored for years came to a screeching halt with the words of the specialist: "Sorry, Becky, there is no possible way for you and your husband to conceive biological children." Zero percent—not even a slight hope to fantasize about!

The infertility testing was discontinued, and we were left with the blunt fact—you are *infertile*. Even the word seemed to mock us. It was such a slap in the face to a couple who desired children as much as we did. I remember wanting to get pregnant on our honeymoon! Now the joy of carrying and birthing a child would never be mine.

I laid in bed alone watching the sun stream in through the window. Yet, only dark questions flooded my consciousness: "Why me, God? What sins have I committed? Didn't I have enough faith to believe?"

Usually, I'm a very energetic person who jumps out of bed and gets going right away. But not this morning. My body was drained of all energy, and I couldn't cry any more. I had no reason to get up even though I had a full-time job. Why go to work just to have everyone ask why my eyes are swollen?

So I lay there helpless, staring aimlessly out the window at the beautiful California scenery that today seemed so bland. Even during the testing, I could at least stay in bed with a thermometer in my mouth, holding onto the slightest hope of someday conceiving a child. But today I was numb, and the question kept racing through my mind, "Why me, God?"

Looking back now, I realize I was just beginning my "grief" period. The news of not being able to have "my own" children was a terrible blow. I had been brought up in a home and society that taught a woman could be fulfilled only if she were married and had children. In fact, I can honestly say that was my number one goal in life.

Now I had to surrender the dream of experiencing natural childbirth, having my husband present during delivery, showing off baby pictures afterwards, and shopping for cute baby clothes with friends. These were things that I longed and lived for. To be denied them was to admit I was only "half a woman."

How do you die to long-held hopes and dreams? How do you go on, knowing that you can't have children? How do you have a relationship with a God who, you feel, has turned His back on you? Why had God chosen *me* to be unable to bear a child?

Questions raced through my mind, and no answers seemed to come. How could I pray to God? Hadn't He allowed this? How could God fail me when I had given my life completely over to Him? Hidden resentment set in.

No Gifts from God

Before marriage, I had prepared myself for service and had been actively involved in ministry. Ray and I were now pastoring one of the largest singles groups in the nation, and

God was performing mighty works through us. We believed in His miraculous power, and the Holy Spirit was actively working in our ministry. But now it seemed God was far away and He couldn't hear us. Or did He just refuse to listen?

This very personal problem was magnified because of our public profile. We felt no liberty to show our grief. One Mother's Day, our gracious senior pastor gave a sermon on how children are "a gift from God." His every word pierced my heart like an arrow. I thought, If children are a gift from God, then infertility must be a curse from God. I burst into tears right in the middle of the service.

Such a response would have been acceptable for a congregational member but not for a pastor's wife. We are viewed as being perfect and never allowing problems to upset us. But that day I could not hold back the tears; it hurt too much.

After the service, one of the singles walked up and told me, "You shouldn't be crying; you're supposed to be an example to us!" So I collected myself, walked out of the sanctuary, and drove home, only to hurl myself onto the bed sobbing uncontrollably.

"Oh God, how could You have done this to me?" I cried. "Why me? I can't even show my emotions because of our ministry. Thousands of people are looking to us for spiritual leadership, and eyes are on us everywhere we go. I can't even go into a bank or store without somebody knowing who I am and asking me why I have tear-stained eyes. Oh God, how can I face life and continue on in ministry?"

I finally got up enough strength to open my Bible, hoping that God would speak to me and relieve my heartache. Yet, all I could find were verses saying that barrenness was considered one of the worst "curses" in the Bible.

God's Word itself degrades a "barren" woman. No wonder most people consider infertility as a sign of God's judgment. Children are a gift from God; therefore, God must be displeased with those who are denied the joy of having them.

In my search that day, I opened to Proverbs 30:15,16, where three things that are never satisfied are listed: the grave, barrenness, and the desert needing water. The Bible describes barrenness and the longing for children as a consuming desire, like a desert thirsting for water. It even declares that as hell desires souls and never has enough, so a woman without children is left wanting. That was exactly how I felt.

I poured out my heart to my heavenly Father, crying and writing down my prayers. It brought me comfort to know He understood the despair and hopelessness I was feeling.

As the days went by, I gradually began accepting our infertility although I still questioned God. It was a rough road with a long way to go.

In my prayer journal I wrote,

> It's been a month now, God, and the hurt is not going away. Something must be wrong with me. The unanswered question, "Why me?" keeps running through my mind—morning, noon, and night. Will it ever go away? I'm worried about the signs of jealousy toward other women and my resentment toward You, Lord. The joy and zeal of my life is gone, and something is missing. I don't see the beauty in my surroundings anymore; I see only ugliness.

Church life is often focused on families. This causes childless couples and singles to feel isolated and left out.

They think if they aren't married and don't have children, then they aren't welcome or don't belong at certain church functions.

With enough determination, I could handle the occasional baby shower or Sunday morning baby dedication, but the once-a-month cycle, when my own body betrayed me, was more difficult. My menstrual period seemed to curse me. I hated the fact that I could not reproduce. I felt like an incomplete woman—a failure.

A childless woman can have very low self-esteem, making her feel inferior to other women. I know the feeling. Every woman you meet has been pregnant at some time in her life. They have all attained that wonderful and valued position of *motherhood.*

On my way to work, I would pass a schoolyard and gaze longingly upon the children playing. Once I almost hit the car in front of me while I was daydreaming and wondering, What would my little girl or little boy look like if I could have one?

In a supermarket when I would see a mother screaming at her children, I want to walk up and say, "If you're not going to treat them right, please give them to me—I would love to have them."

It seems everyone can bear children except you. In the doctor's office you hear women talking about how easily they get pregnant. You pretend not to hear, but the words go straight to the heart.

In the moments I was most vulnerable, God always provided the appropriate help. During a time when my self-worth was at its lowest because of my childlessness, I came across this paraphrase of Psalm 139 written by a woman facing the very battle I felt I was losing. As you read it, you'll see why it brought me encouragement at a time when I most needed it.

Psalm 139
(For The Infertile Woman)
by Gaye Ruschen

Oh Lord, you have searched me and you know me.

You know when I sit and when I rise; you perceive my thoughts from afar.

You know my pain when I hold a friend's newborn child.

You know my joy when I play with the neighborhood children or buy a bright pink and white-striped raincoat for my niece.

You know my love when I brush the long golden hair of a little girl who is a special friend or when I plan small and fun surprises for the children in my Sunday School class.

You know my grief over an adoption that has fallen through or another menstrual cycle that has begun.

You know my desire when I rock a tiny baby to sleep in the church nursery and experience that indescribable warmth that small children spread to those around them.

You are familiar with my ways.

Before a word is on my tongue, you know it completely, O Lord . . .

Even when it is a complaint about taking my basal temperature or my half-hearted agreement to another poking, prying test or surgery.

You hem me in—behind and before; you have laid your hand upon me.

Your loving touch has healed my broken heart when I haven't believed that anything could.

Where can I go from your Spirit?

Where can I flee from your presence?

If I go up to the heavens, you are there.

When I let my optimism carry me to the highest limits of excitement and joy; you are there.

If I make my bed in the depths; you are there.

When my spirit sinks into the pit of self-hatred, self-pity and bitterness; you are there.

If I rise on the wings of the dawn, if I settle on the far side of the sea, even there your hand will guide me, your right hand will hold me fast.

When I deny my desire for a child or when I isolate myself from those who are expecting a baby or have been blessed with children —you are there and you guide me and comfort me.

If I say, "Surely the darkness will hide me and the light become night around me."

Even the darkness will not be dark to you; the night will shine like day, for darkness is as a light to you.

If I say, "I can deal with my infertility by myself without help from God."

I can't fool you, Lord, you know my weakness and patiently wait for me to turn to you for comfort once again.

For you created my inmost being; you knit me together in my mother's womb.

You know how much my mother with a fertility problem of her own desired my conception.

I praise you because I am fearfully and wonderfully made; your works are wonderful, I know that full well.

My frame was not hidden from you when I was made in the secret place.

When I was woven together in the depths of the earth, your eyes saw my unformed body.

They saw the endometriosis, the low progesterone level, the ovaries that wouldn't release a tiny egg each month.

You saw these things and knew that someday they would make my faith in you flourish and strengthen—and that the growing pains along the way would make me love you more each day.

But still I know your creation is wonderfully made.

All the days ordained for me were written in your book before they came to be.

You knew about each biopsy, each x-ray, each negative pregnancy test that would become routine occurrences in my life and the life of my husband.

How precious to me are thy thoughts, O God!

How vast the sum of them! Were I to count them, they would outnumber the grains of sand.

Lord, you love and care for me.

You have blessed my life richly in many ways—
with good friends, a supportive family, a loving
husband and most of all the courage and strength
I receive from you.

When I awake, I am still with you.

And I know that you are always with me.

Cursed by God?

Over and over again, I asked myself, "Am I being cursed
by God?" I knew I had to deal with this thought before it
turned into bitterness and produced serious spiritual
consequences. When I began to seek an answer to this question from God's Word, the truth was revealed to me.

The story in Luke, chapter one, about Zacharias and
Elizabeth had always held special meaning for me. One day,
as I was reading it again and searching for an answer to my
despair, I saw something I had never seen before.

For many years, Zacharias and Elizabeth were unable
to have children. They were upright in the sight of God,
observing *all* of the Lord's commandments. Yet, Elizabeth
couldn't have children. Were they being judged by God?

The Bible says,

Both of them were upright in the sight of God,
observing all the Lord's commandments and regulations blamelessly. But they had no children,
because Elizabeth was barren; and they were both
well along in years (Luke 1:6-7, NIV).

Elizabeth had suffered ridicule and embarrassment for
many years because she had no children. But her barrenness had nothing to do with her relationship to God. In fact,

she and her husband were both righteous and blameless in God's eyes.

When the time finally came for her to conceive, she said, "The Lord has done this for me. In these days he has shown his favor and taken away my disgrace among the people" (Luke 1:25). Elizabeth's disgrace was not with God but with the people. God allowed her to be barren until the time came for His perfect will to be fulfilled.

God doesn't "judge" us with infertility, but He does allow it. Our prayers never go unnoticed by our loving heavenly Father. God always answers prayer, but the answer is sometimes, "Yes"; sometimes, "No"; but most often, He says, "Wait." God cannot always reveal His will to us at the moment we pray because we would not comprehend all His ways.

During this time of searching for answers and reasons, I thought back to the most traumatic experience of my life. While visiting friends, I had been attacked by a vicious German shepherd dog. Before my friends were able to pull him off me, the dog had torn open my face, neck, and hands. I was rushed to the hospital.

As the doctor wrapped my face, he tried to reassure me with the prospect of plastic surgery if the scars were too noticeable. I knew that permanent scarring was inevitable if the wounds did not heal properly.

When the right side of my face became abscessed and the stitches ripped open, the situation looked hopeless. "Who would want to marry me now?" I angrily asked God. Months before the accident I had been struggling with being single and was convinced I must be the most undesirable woman in the whole world. Now my hopes of finding a mate appeared impossible.

After begging, pleading, and demanding that He *do* something, I realized the problem was not God's unwillingness to heal—the real problem was my rebellious attitude. Promising to serve Him even if it meant being single and scarred, I repented. At that moment, the Lord touched me, healing me where I needed it most—on the inside.

The next day I called my pastor and told him of my change of heart. He immediately came over and prayed for me, asking God for a physical healing. Soon the abscesses disappeared, and the skin healed. When I went back to the hospital for my check-up, the doctors and nurses couldn't believe that my face had healed so quickly. God had performed a miracle!

But that wasn't all. Not long after I surrendered to God, Ray and I began seeing one another, and within the year we were married. I came to realize that "with God nothing is impossible."

Now, four years later, as I faced this new crisis in my life, I reflected on God's goodness, knowing that He had not caused our infertility. The hardest part was accepting the fact that He had allowed it. In time, however, I realized that it wasn't my place to ask "why" but to be content and praise Him.

When the question, "Why me, God?" enters your mind, realize immediately that God is not judging you with this problem. Infertility is one of the consequences of living in a fallen world. If infertility were a curse, then most non-Christians would be sterile and this problem wouldn't affect Christians at all. But God "causes his sun to rise on the evil and the good, and sends rain on the righteous and the unrighteous" (Matthew 5:45).

God can and will heal infertility problems. But we should believe God for a miracle without demanding our own way. Ray and I will continue to serve and love Him whether God heals us or not.

We need to learn to trust God as our loving heavenly

Father who always has our best interests and His highest purpose in mind for us. In the chapters ahead, let's look at what should be our proper response to infertility and any other problem we may face in life.

CHAPTER THREE

Discovering Infertility

Infertility is a hot topic. Television talk shows discuss the trauma involved, magazine articles offer advice, and newscasts report the latest developments in infertility research.

In the past there was the occasional childless couple, but today infertility has become a common problem. A recent issue of *Newsweek Magazine* reported that 10%-20% of all American couples have fertility problems. "As many as 3.5 million—about one in five—are infertile."[1]

Although medical research in this area is expanding and new research techniques are being developed, there are no simple solutions. In fact, determining the actual cause of infertility can take several years and involve extensive testing.

Some couples, after only a few months of trying to conceive, get discouraged and begin to wonder if they have a problem. Yet, given a year, 80 percent of women not trying to hinder conception will become pregnant. Of the 20 percent who fail to conceive, 5 percent can be helped through sex counseling, surgery, fertility drugs, and other medical procedures.

Doctors label a couple infertile after one full year of regular, unprotected intercourse. Yet, even without therapy up to 35 percent of these couples conceive within two years.

Once Rebecca and I realized we needed help conceiving a child, we were soon involved in a network of people and specialists we had not known existed: lab technicians who identify infertility, doctors who research solutions, couples who are infertile, and counselors who help you through your problem.

With all the new technology and research in the area of infertility—microsurgery, hormone treatment, laser therapy, ultrasound—it is now possible for 50 to 80 percent of couples considered infertile to achieve a successful pregnancy.[2]

Initial Testing

After a year of attempting conception without success, we suggest that a couple go through the early infertility tests. Get a specialist, and rid yourselves of the haunting question, "What's wrong?" Most problems are diagnosed in the early stages of testing. Only a few cases require the full range, and only a minority discover total infertility.

The truth has a way of destroying fear, anxiety, and stress. And, who knows, there may be a very simple solution to your problem.

At this point let me emphasize the importance of finding a reputable, qualified infertility specialist. Many doctors and gynecologists will try to help you, but their expertise is this area is often limited. Don't waste valuable time and money with an uninformed or insensitive doctor.

Asking questions is your best form of insurance. Quiz your doctor on the type of procedures he uses in resolving infertility and what his success rate has been. It's important that you be well-informed about the kinds of tests available and the procedures involved in treating infertility. If you know the facts, you should be able to discern whether or not your doctor can help you.

A competent infertility specialist will try to eliminate any obvious reasons that may be hampering conception. The following diagnostic tests are usually recommended.

Physical Examination. A routine gynecological examination, if not done previously on the wife, is absolutely necessary. The physician will be able to determine if there are any growths in the uterus (fibroid), tumors on the ovaries, or the presence of endometriosis. Abnormalities in the uterus, vagina, and cervix can also prevent conception.

If there appears to be no obvious reason for the infertility, the physician will suggest certain lab tests to determine the possibility of a vaginal or cervical infection. A blood test will check for anemia or blood problems that could be a factor in infertility. Also, tests for any evidence of kidney or liver disease, diabetes, or thyroid problems should be done.

Temperature Charts. Most physicians will recommend that the wife keep a record of her basal body temperature for a year to determine the time of ovulation each month. Using this method helps isolate the peak point of possible conception and indicates whether the wife is ovulating regularly. Also, an at home ovulation test kit that can be purchased at your local pharmacy will predict when ovulation occurs and help make intercourse more timely.

Using the basal temperature charts kept by the wife and blood tests done at a lab, the physician can determine if ovulation is occurring regularly. If, however, the wife is not having regular periods, charting the basal temperature is of little use. For older couples, it might be best to begin further infertility testing without completing a full year of temperature charts. Twelve months can mean precious time wasted in a battle where the enemy is your own body.

Pinpointing the Problem

If it has been determined that the wife is ovulating regularly but she still has not become pregnant, a spermatozoa analysis on the husband will be recommended. Almost 40 percent of problems with infertility can be traced to the male partner and 40 percent to the female.[3] Many times both partners have some kind of reproductive deficiency. It is much more difficult, however, to successfully treat the infertile man than the infertile woman.

Like many males, I wasn't open to the idea that it might be *my* problem. This is the point at which many couples reach an impasse. The husband is too proud to go for testing, and the wife is often forced to proceed alone. Yet, until the husband has been cleared of having any problems, the doctor or specialist cannot make a certain diagnosis.

We know several couples, most in their middle thirties, who are without children. No one knows why they can't conceive because the husband refuses to go to the doctor. It is the wife, however, who bears the pain and disgrace of childlessness.

The Bible says a husband and wife are *one* flesh. Husbands should love their wives enough to defeat the stubbornness of male pride that says, "I won't go through testing." When one partner is hurting, it is the responsibility of the other to assist in relieving the pain.

Once I realized that it was just as much my responsibility as my wife's to find out what the problem was, I humbled myself and submitted to the semen test. This first in the long battle against infertility tells if the husband has high spermatozoa count, low spermatozoa count, or no spermatozoa at all.

It only took one-half hour, but the most humiliating part was sitting in a cubicle-size bathroom where I had to produce a specimen for testing. A full spectrum of emotions rolled through me. I didn't need someone in particular to be angry at, anyone would do—an orderly passing by or the cold, calculating nurse who labeled the bottle like an assembly line worker. No smiles or thank you's or I hope you're doing okay, yet my whole future seemed to hinge on this test.

I later learned that most specimens can be obtained in the privacy of the home and then taken to the hospital, doctor's office, or lab where the analysis is performed. It is important, in order to obtain a proper specimen, to ask for specific instructions regarding collection and transportation of the specimen. Since this is such a sensitive subject, many lab technicians and office personnel tend to give as few directions as possible. Don't be afraid to ask questions. A few uncomfortable moments obtaining adequate information can save you the time and money expended to take the test over.

When the results of the semen test were completed, they told me I fell into the third category: no spermatozoa at all. That meant further investigation. Male infertility, however, should not be definitely diagnosed on the results of one semen analysis. If the doctor does not recommend another, then make sure you request, or insist, on another test.

Most doctors consider a semen sample normal if it contains 20,000 sperm per milliliter, with 60 percent death rate and 40-60 percent mobility. There are several common causes of poor sperm quality. An enlarged vein in the testicle called a *varicocele* is responsible for 20 to 30 percent of low sperm counts and is correctable by surgery. The sperm-producing cells of the testicle can be damaged by mumps at puberty, and gonorrhea can scar the male reproductive passage.

Environmental factors also affect sperm production. Excessive heat around the scrotum caused by underwear that is too tight, prolonged hot baths, or undescended testicles can reduce sperm production at least temporarily. Low sperm counts can also result from occupational exposure to radiation, lead, or pesticides. Use of marijuana or alcohol may also be responsible. Simple changes in lifestyle can improve sperm quality in only a few months.[4]

Birth defects in the manufacture of or the transport of sperm are sometimes responsible for poor quality. Of men who are tested, only 2 percent are infertile because of a congenital problem. Surgical correction is usually impossible, but artificial insemination of the husband's sperm may result in the wife's pregnancy.

This is only an overview of the most common causes of male infertility. We recommend that you see an infertility specialist to work on your individual problem. He may recommend that the husband see a urologist to help diagnose treatment.

Adding Insult to Injury

I'm grateful we discovered the source of our problem soon enough to pursue other courses of action. It is better to know where you stand than to go on month after month in a cloud of uncertainty. Although it was difficult for me to admit that it was my body disfunctioning, at least we knew where we were, and we knew what to pray about.

Once our problem was pinpointed, it was not necessary for Rebecca to go through a much more complicated battery of tests. My willingness to cooperate in the initial stages saved my wife a lot of physical discomfort and saved us both a great deal of marital and financial stress. We could now focus on what could be done for my problem.

A compassionate infertility specialist took charge of our case and made the duration of testing easier. He told me I would be admitted as an out-patient, checking in at 6:00 a.m., and free to go home by 5:00 p.m. Two techniques would be used. First, a surgical probe would check out the *vas deferens tube* through which the semen travels. Then a testicle biopsy (dasography) would be performed.

At the time, Rebecca and I were the pastors of a large singles ministry that we had developed from only a handful to over eight hundred in attendance weekly. We knew people in every walk of life.

When I was undergoing the surgical probe, the location of my surgery (mid-section) required that I be absolutely naked on the table. I was totally exposed. That was difficult enough, but to make matters worse, the anesthesiologist and the main surgical nurse were members of my singles ministry. I laid there, infertile and totally exposed, before people who looked to me as their spiritual leader.

When I awoke from the general anesthesia, the doctor told me that no biopsy was necessary. They discovered that the vas deferens was not fully developed; it just ended at one point.

Simple enough, I thought. Just take the sperm from where the tube ends and artificially inseminate it into my wife's body. We're one, it's not like using a sperm bank. I later learned that the sperm develops into maturity while traveling through the tube, and they're not mature until they have completed the course.

Since no incisions had been made during the probe, I was released from the hospital earlier than expected. On the way home, my mind was full of the experience and the facts. Walking up my driveway, I suddenly became nauseated from the general anesthesia and vomited right in the front yard. Crouched on all fours, I was now humiliated before the whole neighborhood by this repulsive act. I had truly hit the lowest point in my life.

Medically, there was no solution to my problem. It would take a miracle for us to have biological children. At that point no more testing was necessary.

A physical healing would have solved my problem, but God had a higher purpose in mind. During the period of infertility testing, God was shaping my character in a new way. At the time, however, every new incident seemed to add insult to injury.

Female Infertility Testing

While the male system involves only the sperm and the tubes that transport them, the female system is much more complicated. While we will not go into detail about all the problems concerning female infertility, we will discuss the most common.

If the husband has undergone a semen analysis and his sperm count is normal, the infertility specialist will suggest that the wife go through a battery of tests. Commencing with the simplest, these tests become more expensive and complicated until the source of the problem is located. Although Rebecca did not have to go through these tests, we would like to include them for your information.

Postcoital Test. Sometimes the wife's cervical mucus is too thick to be penetrated by the sperm, or the mucus may be hostile to the sperm, causing it to die. To determine this, the couple will be asked to have sexual relations just prior to rushing off to a scheduled appointment with the infertility specialist. The doctor will take a sample of the wife's mucus and examine it under the microscope to see how it responds to the husband's sperm. This test is also called the Sims-Huhner test.

Your physician can often prescribe a simple but effective treatment that will eliminate any problems involving cervical mucus. For this reason, make sure your physician recommends this test before going on to the more complicated (and expensive) tests that we will discuss next.

Endometrial Biopsy. In order to determine whether ovulation is taking place and if the progesterone level is normal, your specialist will perform an endometrial biopsy in which a sample of tissue is scraped off the lining of the uterus. While this procedure is often done in the doctor's office it can be quite painful. Women who have had this test done suggest that it is better to combine the endometrial biopsy with a laparoscopy (which we will discuss next).

About 20 percent of all infertility is due to the wife's hormone imbalance that affects ovulation. Several drugs, including Clomid and Pergonal, are available to treat hormonal problems. According to *Newsweek* magazine, "About half the women whose infertility is caused by hormonal problems can achieve pregnancy with treatment by drugs like these."[5]

Pergonal, however, can sometimes overstimulate the ovaries, resulting in multiple births.

Test for Tubal and Uterine Problems. Each month the egg produced by a woman's body must travel through the fallopian tubes in order for conception to take place. Tubes that are scarred, twisted, or knotted as a result of infection hamper fertility. Many infertile women have endometriosis, an abnormal growth of tissue around the reproductive organs and inside the fallopian tubes.

Endometriosis is diagnosed using a process called laparoscopy in which the physician views the affected area through a tube inserted through an abdominal incision. If the condition is not far advanced, the physician can remove the abnormal tissue at the time of the laparoscopy.

Because general anesthesia is used during this procedure, it is a good time to have the endometrial biopsy performed as well. It is important that both these procedures be done as soon as possible so that treatment can be started. Some problems can be repaired simply, while extensive damage requires a major abdominal operation.

One woman said her first infertility specialist took a full year to recommend and complete the endometrial biopsy and laparoscopy. When she started going to a new specialist, he performed the same procedures in one day. But a precious year had already been lost because her first doctor was inexperienced.

We suggest that women abstain from intercourse and have a pregnancy test taken prior to having these procedures performed to prevent an abortion from taking place at the time.

Information—Your Best Defense

The medical field of infertility is changing rapidly, and new discoveries are made every year. Read every article you can find on the subject, and don't be afraid to discuss new procedures with your doctor. Laser treatments for endometriosis and microsurgery for repairing tubal damage are becoming more and more common.

In the book, *Dear God, Why Can't We Have A Baby?* by John and Sylvia Van Regenmorter, their co-author Dr. Joe S. McIlhaney, Jr. provides detailed information on the different tests for infertility. Written from a Christian perspective, their advice is most helpful.

Insurance companies are more readily accepting infertility medical procedures as normal illness. Such was not the case a few years ago. It is imperative that you clearly check your coverage before blindly moving ahead. Each test becomes more complicated and expensive. If the full battery of tests is required, the cost could escalate to nearly $10,000—and this price does not include treatment.

We were grateful to have learned about the nature of our problem in the early stages of testing. Although our insurance company covered the bill, we would gladly have paid for the tests ourselves. We feel children are worth any price. If, however, the order of testing had been wrong, the costs could have increased in spite of the fact that our problem was fairly easy to discover.

This is no time to fool around with uninformed practitioners. Research, read, and ask a lot of questions. Before undergoing expensive surgery, I suggest you look into some of the simple solutions offered to you by specialists. I have read of various infertility problems being solved quite easily by taking vitamins or hormones and using baking soda douches, etc.

In *Prevention Magazine*, I read about a man who was suffering from a low sperm count.[6] Some of his sperm were irregularly formed, others were immature and incapable of fertilization. He also had a varicose vein in the testicle.

This man was told to have surgery although there was only a fifty-fifty chance of its being successful. He decided to do some research before going ahead with the procedure. After going to a nutritionist, he was put on vitamins for four months. When another analysis was done, his sperm had a high normal count and were fully active. His wife became pregnant as a result.

I am not advocating that vitamins are the answer to every problem, but I want to encourage you to pray, seek God's wisdom in this matter, and research every possible avenue of treatment before submitting yourself to expensive and unguaranteed procedures. Make sure your doctor informs you of any and all possible side-affects or damage that might result from surgery or drug treatment.

Upon discovering my lack of sperm in the semen, the specialists suggested I go to Houston for experimental surgery. They wanted to place a sack to collect the sperm spilling into my body then artificially inseminate it in my wife's uterus. Research showed this procedure worked once in fifty times. Our insurance company said a hearty "no" to coverage for the surgery. After Rebecca and I prayed about it, we felt we should pursue another direction.

CHAPTER FOUR

Dealing with the Problem

Insensitive people often ask childless couples ridiculous questions: "Becky, why don't you have any little ones yet?" "Don't you love or want children?"

Worse than the callous inquirers are the false prophets of doom who pronounce their opinions without any thought to your feelings. "God doesn't want you to have children or you'd have them!" Or, "Anyone who can't have children must have serious spiritual problems."

We tried not to blame these people for their ignorance, but their words hurt us deeply. It's easy to let resentment and bitterness creep into our lives because of the unthoughtful things other people say and do.

In our counseling with infertile couples, Ray and I always hear the same complaint: How do you respond to the unkind remarks that people express? Couples struggling with infertility must learn to handle the insensitivity and well-intentioned, but often unhelpful, advice of others.

What do you say to the mother-in-law who is always telling you to "relax" and "stop trying so hard"? What about the neighbor who knows five women who got pregnant after they adopted? The myth that adoption cures infertility is just that—a myth. The fact is that spontaneous cures occur in about 5 percent of infertility cases, but they occur no more frequently among those who do not adopt.

Often the best response to insensitive questions is no response at all. People soon get the idea that their comment didn't set very well with you. Be honest without being rude. Tell them how you feel and how much it hurts.

A simple word of explanation can head off uneasiness and misunderstanding. I personally didn't make a secret of our infertility. Because of our ministry, Ray and I often traveled together to speaking engagements. Many times people would ask, "How many children do you have?"

I would respond by saying, "My husband and I can't have children, and we are trusting God to either provide a miracle through healing or a miracle through adoption." I seldom had to say anything more, and the subject was never mentioned again.

It is equally important, however, not to hurt the inquirers feelings either. Usually their remarks are made without any evil intended; they are just said without thinking. Remember, we all put our foot in our mouth at times. The comments people make reflect where they are in life and what they have gone through. If they have never faced infertility, they really don't know what you are experiencing—so don't expect them to.

This fact became clear to me when my brother had his eye gouged out while playing basketball. Being blind in one eye was a shocking and terrible experience for him. I attempted to counsel and console him, but everything I said seemed to hurt him more.

I finally told him, "I wish I could understand what you are going through, but I don't." I stopped trying to be his counselor and started praying for and loving him. In time, the trauma of the incident lessened, and today he is doing remarkably well.

Inner healing doesn't happen overnight. We should allow ourselves time to adjust to the reality of our infertility. Meanwhile, don't get upset with others who are doing the best they can with the knowledge they have.

There is no need to be defensive. Don't take every remark personally; instead give each one to the Lord. Try not to let grudges develop or walls build up that could destroy relationships.

Your Support System

At this point in your life, you need friends. Don't let friendships diminish because you think they can't understand your problem. No matter how strong you feel you are in your inner man or how invincible your marriage, everyone needs help. Regularly spend time with someone who is capable of speaking the truth to you in love. (See Ephesians 4:15.)

A true friend will keep you on track when you're headed toward a danger zone. They can also become your prayer partner, standing with you until victory comes. I know women in our church who have become best friends because they both had a hard time getting pregnant. Great support comes from those who share similar struggles and bear one another's burdens.

Many women have miscarried a child, but miscarriage is not a form of infertility. Those who miscarry are capable of conception but are unable to carry the pregnancy full term. While these women share the same emotional pain and psychological distress as those who cannot conceive, there is a difference. They still have the hope of being able to conceive a child and carry that child full term. An infertile woman has to die to any hope of ever being able to have children. Women who miscarry should not try to counsel those with an infertility problem.

Several good books have been written on the subject of miscarriage. Ann Kiemel Anderson shares her heartbreaking experience in *Taste of Tears/Touch of God*. The book, *Empty Arms* by Pam Vredevelt, offers emotional support for those who have suffered miscarriage or stillbirth. (Also see resources in the *Suggested Reading* under Miscarriage.)

While a prayer partner can be a great blessing, don't allow yourself to become too dependent on someone other than your husband. During this time, you and your spouse need to look to one another for support and comfort. When you pour out your heart to another woman, you may end up sharing things that only your husband needs to hear. The last thing you need is for your husband to feel left out and rejected.

Remember also that men are very private people and don't like to have their personal affairs openly discussed. When sharing with others, be careful not to overstep the bounds of secrecy unique to your marital relationship. It might be a good idea to keep your husband informed about what you have been sharing with your friend. He can then express what he wants to keep only between you, him, and the doctor.

Soul Searching

During the church service one Sunday morning, our senior pastor declared from the pulpit, "How blessed we are for His children and grandchildren, the purest sign of God's blessing."

Following the service, Ray and I made our way through the narrow corridor that linked the sanctuary to the pastors' offices. Every Sunday, all the pastors on staff and their families would gather for a time of fellowship. That day as we walked into the crowded room, it seemed each pastoral family had fifteen kids. With the words of the sermon still ringing in our ears, we sat there childless— the clear proof of God's judgment and lack of blessing in our lives.

Ray and I spent the afternoon at home in soul-searching conversation, looking for anything in our lives that was sinful. I cried while Ray sat emotionless. He was helpless to console me, especially since he felt the infertility was his problem.

I know it hurt him to see me grieving so. "Maybe I was never supposed to get married!" he said. "Perhaps, the Lord will take me home soon, and you will have another chance at family life." The afternoon became the evening, and Ray went to church alone, leaving me to calm my emotions and sort out my feelings.

During the days that followed, many friends and counselors told us we were under judgment. "Discover the sin, and healing will take place," they said. We searched our souls day after day, relinquishing every self-created, sinful attitude.

Indirectly, our senior pastor seemed to be telling us the same thing by declaring children as the purest indicator of God's blessing. What he said was true and absolutely biblical, but it does not apply to every person. It was an innocent declaration of his spiritual excitement, but the enemy used it against us.

Satan wanted us to get bitter over our infertility problem and destroy our relationship with God. Ephesians 6:12 tells us, "For our struggle is not against flesh and blood, but against the rulers, against the authorities, against the powers of this dark world and against the spiritual forces of evil in the heavenly realms."

Jesus said, "The thief comes only to steal and kill and destroy" (John 10:10). Satan wanted to destroy our faith and our testimony. As the accuser of the brethren (Revelation 12:10) and the father of lies (John 8:44), he did everything possible to make us feel condemned, guilty, and resentful.

When we were most vulnerable, Satan attacked and filled our minds with filthy lies:

"God has cursed you with this. He's punishing you for something."

"You are a loser, a failure, a sinner. That's why this evil was placed on you."

"God isn't faithful; He doesn't love you."

"You might as well give up living; this problem will never go away."

"Give up on God, why minister for Him if He won't do this one simple thing for you?"

"Nobody cares. If they did, they'd call and see how you are doing. Why don't you give up on all your Christian friends?"

"Why ask God to heal others? He won't heal your problem."

In the beginning of our struggle, Satan's tactics worked—especially on me. I was starting to believe his lies. Then out of desperation, I turned to God's Word for help. I read James 4:7: "Submit yourselves, then, to God. Resist the devil, and he will flee from you." I had to openly rebuke Satan, and take authority over his interference in my life.

Once I was able to diffuse Satan's lies, I then had to put the first part of that verse into practice. I submitted myself to God and turned to His Word for comfort and guidance.

Dealing with Depression

Facing the reality of infertility can cause deep depression. When there seems to be no possible solution, a sense of helplessness generates an attitude of hopelessness. Infertility is like a death—like losing a child we never had.

The Bible says that Hannah was so depressed over her barrenness that she often wept openly and could not eat. Her husband asked her, "Hannah, why are you weeping? Why don't you eat? Why are you downhearted? Don't I mean more to you than ten sons?" (1 Samuel 1:8).

In spite of her husband's attempt to comfort her, "in bitterness of soul Hannah wept much and prayed to the Lord" (verse 10).

Depression indicates that something is wrong. Many times our emotions indicate a truth about our inner person that God wants to deal with. The hurt and depression you feel, however, are not the turning point. It is your *response* to those feelings that becomes the ledge from which you plummet to new lows or the platform from which you leap to new growth and success.

During this time of grieving, my relationships with others were strained—with my husband, my fellow workers, my friends, and people in our ministry. I didn't want to be around anyone. My depression made it difficult for me to do routine household tasks like cooking, cleaning, and washing clothes.

I just had to get away to contemplate what was going on in my life. At the time, Ray was out of town for a crusade, so I rented a cabin in the mountains and had a friend drop me off. I had no food or transportation. My only objective was to hear from God. If I'm locked in, I thought, God will have to speak to me.

During my stay I was able to cry out to God in my own way. I pounded the floor, stayed up all night, and poured out my heart. This was a good way to release my grief.

Although God didn't speak in an audible voice and I didn't receive answers to most of my questions, my inner peace returned as my relationship with the Father was restored. I now accepted my infertility and chose to go on with life.

Ray, on the other hand, had buried himself in his work, hoping to erase the reality of the fact that he could never father his own children. When I returned, I shared my experience with him. He finally agreed that we should go away together to pray and discuss our feelings with one another.

As we cried out to God, Ray and I were drawn closer together. Although God didn't give us the answer we were wanting, He did give us a peace in our hearts that later produced an inner healing. This was our first step on the road to recovery.

When depression comes, you may be nearing the point of resolution; but remember—*don't follow your feelings!* Rash decisions made in the pit of despair usually result in greater frustration and pain.

At a low point in her life, Abraham's wife Sarah forgot God's promise and acted on her feelings. The result created strife and animosity in her family life that had long-lasting consequences. (See Genesis chapter 16.)

When you're in the midst of the storm, hold the helm of the boat and keep a steady course until the crisis feelings subside. Learn to react like Jonah, who said, "In my distress I called to the Lord, and he answered me" (Jonah 2:2).

The Father knew the crisis before it began, and He is anxiously waiting for the opportunity to step in to comfort and guide. Remember the promise of Jesus Himself, "I will never leave you nor forsake you." You're not in this alone. You have your spouse and the comforting Holy Spirit. Yours is a position of victory not defeat. You're a victor not a victim.

A Change of Heart

While Ray and I were attending a pastors' seminar, we were called to repentance in every area of our lives. Deep within me I knew that my faith was on shaky ground. I told Ray, "I don't believe God for the big miracles anymore." A small seed of bitterness had developed, dampening my faith in God to do the impossible for myself and for others.

The Lord also convicted me of a serious attitude problem. I read in the Bible that Rachel was jealous of her sister Leah because she had several children and Rachel had none. (See Genesis chapters 29-30.) Jealousy had gripped my heart, too. Whenever possible I avoided being around young mothers, and I found myself envying those who could have children.

I needed to address the negative attitudes that infertility had produced in me. As I confessed my sin and poured my heart out to God, He forgave me and healed my inner being. Then, He went a step further and dug out an attitude that had plagued not only our infertility but my entire spiritual life as well.

I felt I had a *right* to have children. But the Lord showed me that as believers, we are God's possession; we are no longer our own. God's Word says that we are bought with a price (1 Corinthians 6:20). When we presume to know what God should be doing in a particular situation and insist that He do it that way, we are on the verge of serious spiritual rebellion.

Finally, I yielded all my rights to God. I told Him I would serve Him just the way things were—with or without children. Once I submitted to my heavenly Father, a spiritual freedom came into my life that still continues today.

Before God can move to change a situation, He first wants

to deal with our attitudes and heal our hearts. But we must be honest with Him and with ourselves.

When God seems far away, we need to ask Him to show us anything in our lives that is blocking our relationship with Him. God is faithful to instruct us if our hearts are open to the searchlight of His Holy Spirit. With gentleness and compassion, He will lead us into the truth. As we submit to His workings in our life and let Him deal with any wrong attitudes or harmful emotions, God's forgiveness will bring the healing that sets us free.

The Power of Praise and Trust

Few people have had the extremes of successes and failures that King David had. While the Psalms that David wrote act as a mirror in which we see our own weak and sinful humanity, they can also be a magnifying glass in which we see God's way of overcoming great obstacles. Maybe that's why the two key themes of the Psalms are *trust in the Lord* (Psalm 37) and *praise to God* (Psalm 100).

Praise had always been an important part of our spiritual lives, but it was not so easy to praise and worship God when our greatest desire was unfulfilled. In the depths of despair, Ray and I focused our hopes on the words of the thirty-seventh psalm:

> Do not fret . . . Trust in the Lord . . . Delight your-
> self in the Lord and he will give you the desires
> of your heart . . . Commit your way to the Lord
> . . . Be still before the Lord and wait patiently for
> him . . . Refrain from anger and turn from wrath
> . . . Those who hope in the Lord will inherit the
> land . . . The days of the blameless are known to
> the Lord . . . The Lord loves the just and will

not forsake his faithful ones . . . Consider the blameless, observe the upright; there is a future for the man of peace . . . The salvation of the righteous comes from the Lord; he is their stronghold in time of trouble.

These verses from Psalm 37 helped us trust God and His perfect plan for our lives. Although the final outcome was still a mystery, we were able to praise Him because we believed He had everything under control.

God's Word makes praise a mandate:

Rejoice in the Lord always. I will say it again: Rejoice! . . . Do not be anxious about anything, but in everything, by prayer and petition, with thanksgiving, present your requests to God. And the peace of God, which transcends all understanding, will guard your hearts and your minds in Christ Jesus (Philippians 4:4-7).

There is power in praise! To praise Him is to make Him (Jesus Christ) supreme Lord. The best antidote for a broken heart and the negative works of the enemy is *praise*. It disarms and deactivates all that stands against your doing the will of God. Praise eliminates other signals and enables you to hear clearly that tender but quiet voice of God.

As you praise Him, the Father will minister peace that allows you to put your marriage, emotions, and family into His care. Pure praise demonstrates trust. When we can praise God in the midst of trouble, we focus on the Creator and His plan—not on the created and its problem.

Ray and I began to daily praise God in the situation. Whenever the problem of infertility started to overwhelm us, we responded toward the Lord with thanksgiving. Many times we had to bring "the sacrifice of praise," worshiping God with our *will* until our heart followed suit. It drew us closer together and nearer to God as we entered "His courts with praise."

When Healing Comes

Inner healing for such a traumatic and delicate matter as infertility is a process that requires time. But it *will* come. Here are a few signposts that indicate you are on the road to recovery.

Healing is taking place in your life when:

1. *You no longer blame God or doubt His love for you.* When I was able to say, "Lord, I trust You with this. Have Your own way," then I knew my relationship with God had been restored and strengthened.

2. *You can praise the Lord in the present and trust Him for the future.* Whenever I was hurting or doubting, I would force myself to praise God. I knew I was healed when the praises flowed, and the hurt and doubts were gone.

3. *You are able to diffuse Satan's lies by resisting him with the power of God's Word.* When negative thoughts would come into my mind, I learned to say to them and to myself, "That's not true. God is in control of my life, and He knows what is best for me."

4. *You can openly admit and discuss what happened.* I knew healing had occurred when it was no longer difficult for me to say, "We have an infertility problem." In fact, I can now talk openly about what we went through and how we are dealing with it today.

5. *You can minister to others who are hurting.* Final healing came for me when I was able to let God use what I had experienced—the grief, the depression, the bitterness, the anger, the humiliation—to help someone else deal with the pain in her life.

This poem by Denise Majewski bridges the gap between letting God heal you and being sensitive to others.

Don't Let Me Forget, Lord!

Dear Lord!

If ever I am given the privilege of having a child, please don't let me forget this road I have traveled.

Don't let me forget the tears that have been shed, the long restless nights, the longings of the heart.

Don't let me forget the pain—both physical and emotional, or the times when I needed so badly to hear someone say, "I care" or "Do you need to talk about it?"

Don't let me forget the times of quiet reflection, the lessons you taught me in patience, coping, understanding and faith.

Most of all, dear Father, don't let me forget how you were always there for me even when I rejected your peace and love.

Lord, help me to remember all of these things, so that if ever someone I know has to travel this same road, they won't be as alone as I have been.

I will be able to say to them, "I don't know where your road ends, but I do know that the way is rough and I will be your friend on the journey."

Lord, don't let me forget.

In Jesus' Name,

AMEN

CHAPTER FIVE

Options and Alternatives

Looking out the window of a Boeing 727 could convince anyone God is alive and well. The sun's golden reflection on the nimbus clouds creates a layer that looks like glistening snow. Thrilled by the majesty of the moment makes me want to open the window and shout my thoughts, knowing they will glide along the clouds and arrive at God's throne. I have no doubt that His response will return clearly and distinctly to my open heart.

I wish all plane trips for Ray Larson were so positive. In fact, a 1981 trip in a similar jet, with similar purposes in mind, could not have been more opposite. The sky was turbulent, the food was inferior, and I was miserable. Isn't is amazing how the circumstances in our lives can reflect our inner struggle?

While flying, I was asking God for answers. "What do we do now, Lord?" After all, God had allowed our infertility, hadn't He? Then He must, as well, know the course of action we needed to take. Do we pursue more medical help? Do we wait for a miracle?

What I really wanted was a personal answer from God—an audible voice, angelic visitation, or whatever—as long as it came *now*! Does the clay say to the potter,"Father give me an answer before this jet lands"?

Looking back, I can see that my attitude toward God was dangerously poisoned with resentment. I couldn't have heard God speak even if He had been shouting to me—and He might have been. His voice couldn't penetrate my own barrier of bitterness.

A multitude of counselors (many of whom didn't love or even believe in God) had offered confusing and conflicting advice. Through them the enemy was trying to introduce his opinion of the situation and his *many*, many courses of action. His objective was to send voices that would scramble the signal from God.

On a football team the other ten members of an offense wait patiently as the quarterback shouts out signals. They have been given a sequence of numbers that will commence the play. Often the opposing team's defense shouts numbers and words to provoke a premature response. If the players, however, focus in on the quarterback's voice and remind themselves of the right signal, its arrival will unleash a unified effort that can spur them toward victory.

Rebecca and I knew God's promises and had heard His voice, but everyone else was barking conflicting signals. Unfortunately, we let the opposition throw us off balance.

Scrambled Signals

Many alternatives are available to the infertile couple— artificial insemination, embryo transfer, in vitro fertilization, surrogate motherhood, adoption. It's amazing how easy it is to accept the opinions of the world in a moment of inner conflict. Some of their ideas, which I would have preached against before this encounter and would again now, seemed rather attractive at the time.

During our crisis, advice from other people flooded our circumstance. From every direction came a new slant or a different perspective. Most of these people loved us deeply and sincerely wanted to offer solace and solution. Their advice, however, only scrambled the signals, making it hard for us to hear God clearly.

Many times, when clarity seemed to be coming, a new approach to the problem would surface. All these people meant well, but as long as we listened to them instead of God, confusion reigned.

The book of Job describes the crisis that befell this great man of God. His friends came to diagnose the problem and to offer solutions. These men had good intentions and loved Job deeply. This is proven by the distance they traveled to visit their hurting compatriot. Nonetheless, their information and approach offered no relief to Job's misery.

The Bible clearly says, "Many advisers make victory sure" (Proverbs 11:14). But a wise counselor must be informed on the subject and spiritually in tune with God before confronting the situation. The latter chapters of the book of Job reveal the error in the counsel he received. In fact, Job was called upon to pray for these men that they might be forgiven by God.

One well-meaning believer told us our infertility was an indication we were never intended to be married. Fortunately, God had already dealt with our hearts about this matter. We *were* married and intended to stay that way until death parted us or Jesus Christ returned.

The advice we heard was as diverse as the people who gave it. The most humorous came from a couple who were our dearest friends. They said, "Forget all the medical hubbubery. Pray before having relations, then immediately after having sex Becky should go stand on her head for ten minutes." This was supposed to take care of everything. They never explained their advice, and we never asked.

We did, however, attempt to follow some of the non-christian counsel we received. Like Abraham and Sarah, we became desperate and sought human alternatives to godly solutions. Because of God's grace, we are not being forced to live out our mistakes today. God protected us and loved us through the whole time of misleading advice and willful disobedience to His plan.

Finally, Rebecca and I decided to seek God's will and do some research. Some of the counsel given to us prior to this time had been valuable. As we sought God, He began to deal with several different issues, which we will address later. Through our research and God's counsel, many of the alternatives became clear and understandable to us. We were then able to categorize and pray about each one.

Some of the alternatives we are going to present to you are dangerous—both emotionally and spiritually—but it is important to be aware of that potential. It is essential to pray and seek God's advice and walk in the fullness of what He says to you. God has perfect answers and perfect approaches.

If you get past the scrambled signals and eliminate the ill-advised counsel, God's will for you will gradually become clear. Here are some of the options you may want to consider. We suggest you study each one carefully.

Childfree Living

Once a Christian couple faces the reality of infertility and begins considering the options available, they must take into account God's call on their lives and their own unique situation. God has a special calling on each person and family. Perhaps a ministry call is coming your way that will best be accomplished if there are no children in your home.

The apostle Paul urged men and women to remain unmarried to fulfill this unique calling. (See 1 Corinthians chapter 7.) In those days, if you got married, you had children. Birth control was unheard of. Paul knew that the time and energy required for a family are great.

God calls some to give up the right to have children, allowing Him to fulfill His purpose in their lives. This is not an easy calling and must be carefully discerned. Not everyone is called to be single all their lives, and even fewer are asked to remain childless in marriage. (See Matthew 19:11,12.)

God assigns lifestyles so we may most effectively serve the cause of His kingdom and walk in abundant life. Both husband and wife must come to this conclusion together through prayer and godly guidance.

If you feel that childfree living is your assignment, it should be confirmed in God's Word, through wise spiritual counsel, and an inner witness in your own spirit. If it is God's will, peace will pervade this decision. (See Romans 14:17.) The result of your obedience will be lifelong satisfaction and fulfillment doing the will of God.

When Rebecca and I realized that the medical possibility of our having children was practically nil and the waiting list for adopting a child was an average of five years, we were forced to ask a hard question: "Father, will Your destiny for our lives best be served in a childfree home?" We sought the counsel of God and others for several months, but the fact kept reemerging that God wanted us to raise a family.

If you are at this point in your married life, let me suggest you take the following steps: First, lay down your right to bear and raise children. If, however, you have a strong desire to be a parent, tell the Lord how you feel. He is the One who put that desire within you. Next, ask the Holy Spirit to confirm your decision with Scripture and counsel from other godly Christians. Last, go to your local church leadership and tell them how you feel God is leading you. Let them join in your quest.

Using supernatural methods, God will guide your steps and fill your heart with faith as you see Him answer.

Medical Options

If, after praying and seeking the Lord, you decide that it is God's will for you to be parents, at least you know the ultimate destination of your search. But just as you turn this fork in the road you enter an intersection with paths going in every direction. It is at this point that the Christian couple must look carefully at each possible avenue.

The many medical options available branch off in several directions. In their book, *Dear God, Why Can't We Have A Baby?*, John and Sylvia Van Regenmorter and Joe S. McIlhaney Jr., M.D., present these options in detail. If you are seriously considering a medical alternative, we encourage you to read their book and those they recommend for further research. They cover not only the medical procedures used but the moral implications of each and what they feel should be the Christian response.

For our purposes, we will briefly look at several options and discuss the pros and cons.

Reproductive Surgery. Science has come a long way, and there are several surgical procedures that can help a woman conceive. Doctors are often able to locate a fallopian tube blockage or a tube malfunctioning. Corrective surgery can often repair the damage, resulting in a normal pregnancy.

Medical research has been less successful in helping the male. Two or three kinds of experimental surgery were offered to us, but the success rates were very low. We felt this was not the direction for us to take, but it is worth researching.

Be sure to get as much information as possible about the percentages of success and any side effects of the surgery.

Artificial Insemination. In this procedure, sperm is injected into the wife's vagina or uterus by artificial means. There are two major types of artificial insemination: *AIH* uses a specimen of the husband's sperm that has been collected; *AID* uses sperm from an unrelated, anonymous donor stored in a sperm bank. Both of these methods are being highly recommended and publicized in the media.

While some people believe that this impersonal method takes away from the marital union, we have no problem with using the husband's sperm for insemination if there is a medical problem.

Using sperm from an anonymous donor, however, raises several moral and emotional questions. Is it actually committing adultery, since a third party becomes involved in the marriage relationship? What about the husband's feelings? How does he deal with the fact that his wife is carrying a child conceived with someone else's sperm? What kind of strain does this place on the marriage and the husband's feelings toward the child?

Artificial insemination rarely succeeds on the first try. It often requires six or seven attempts and usually costs several hundred dollars for each try. A couple can spend thousands of dollars for success—if any.

There are mixed opinions from Christian leaders regarding artificial insemination. You need to carefully examine, research, and pray before proceeding with this procedure.

Embryo Transfer. *Newsweek Magazine*, August 1983, released a story about a newly developed method of ovum transfer as a solution for infertility. The sperm of the husband is planted into the uterus of a third party until conception. Then, with a special medical instrument the fertilized egg is removed from the third party and placed into the uterus of the wife. UCLA recently attempted this procedure with a group of fourteen donors; two pregnancies resulted.

The doctors will tell you this is a beneficial approach because the baby develops in the wife's womb, allowing her an emotional and physical link with the baby. But once again, we have the problem of a third party being involved. This method raises controversial issues that must be thoroughly and carefully examined from a scriptural perspective.

Ovum transfer is seldom successful on the first try and may involve many attempts. Whenever a fertilized embryo is removed and not implanted, for one reason or another, the procedure is equal to performing an abortion. For those of us who believe that life begins at conception, this method is out of the question.

In Vitro Fertilization. In 1978 the procedure for producing a test-tube baby was first successfully developed. Today clinics throughout the country perform in vitro fertilization. Although this method brought hope to thousands of infertile women, the success rate remains a disappointing 20 percent.

This procedure involves having the woman take a fertility drug that will cause her to produce more than one egg that month. These eggs are then removed from the body and with precise timing fertilized in a sterile dish, using sperm from the husband or another donor. The embryos grow in a sterile dish for several days before being placed into the woman's uterus.

Although several eggs are fertilized and implanted, not all of them survive. Some die in the dish; others die in the womb. Many pro-life groups oppose this procedure because some embryos are rejected or discarded. Multiple births are also a possibility with this method. If you consider in vitro fertilization, be sure you are aware of every detail involved in this procedure.

In vitro fertilization costs several thousand dollars for each attempt. In most cases more than one attempt is required, and the success rate varies from clinic to clinic.

The magazine, *Science*, March 1985, reports a new method developed at the University of Texas in San Antonio. This new procedure is quick and less expensive but still carries dangerous side effects that need to be researched.

Many Christians find test-tube babies a less controversial solution to infertility because it does not involve a third party. We must advise, once again, as in all procedures, to seek counsel and be sure God has led you every step of the way.

Gamete Intrafallopian Transfer (GIFT). This procedure is similar to in vitro fertilization. Eggs are surgically extracted from the woman's ovaries and drawn into a tube along with the husband's sperm. The contents of the tube are then inserted into one or both of the woman's fallopian tubes. In this way, conception occurs naturally, and the embryos then pass into the uterus where a normal pregnancy results. Any embryos that do not develop normally are passed out as an early miscarriage.

While this method offers a more natural approach than fertilization in a sterile dish, the problem of using several fertilized eggs remain.

Surrogate Mothers

In recent years, the news media has played up court cases surrounding the use of surrogate mothers. The legal ramifications regarding this means of obtaining a baby is only one aspect that must be considered by the childless couple.

The medical procedure involves taking sperm from the

husband and implanting it into the uterus of the surrogate mother. She then becomes pregnant, delivers the baby, and turns the child over to the couple who paid her for her services.

One of the common justifications for this type of artificial insemination is, "Well, at least, the child will be related to one of us." Be careful about that kind of thinking. It is deceptive and can open up a pandora's box of problems. First, there is no guarantee as to who actually fathered the child. Second, the wife is emotionally and physically isolated from the entire procedure. Third, the surrogate mother often develops an attachment to the child that is impossible to break.

Pastor Jack Hayford, writing in *Charisma* magazine, says in his article, "A Christian View of Surrogate Motherhood": "Surrogate parenting tends to deify our will; it removes providence from family planning. . . . I contend family planning is our responsibility within the guidelines that God has set down in His Word."[1]

Any Christian couple considering this method should research the moral and ethical questions it raises. In addition, the long-term consequences and effects on the marriage and the child need to be seriously taken into account.

Involving a Third Party

Sometimes we are too anxious to wait for a resolution to our current need. When that urgency is combined with an exaggerated confidence in the ability of medical science to conquer our problem, the result is often a hasty, but disastrous, decision.

God's Word says, "Do not be anxious about anything, but in everything, by prayer and petition, with thanksgiving, present your requests to God. And the peace of God, which transcends all understanding, will guard your hearts and minds in Christ Jesus" (Philippians 4:6,7). If there was ever a time when you needed to guard your heart, it's at the point of decision.

Before deciding on any medical procedure, it is imperative that you receive a word of guidance from Scripture and have the confirmation of wise, spiritual counsel that releases you to move ahead with peace and assurance. Don't allow yourselves to make a quick decision because you have an immediate need. You may live to regret it.

In Genesis 16:2, we read about the heartbreak of Sarah, the childless wife of Abraham, and their human attempt to fulfill God's promise to them. Taking matters into their own hands, they used another woman, Hagar the slave, to conceive and bear a son for Abraham. But the family strife and heartbreak that resulted proved they had stepped out of God's perfect will for their lives.

Research the options, think about what you are doing, consider why you want children. Talk to your infertility specialist and get many opinions about your particular problem. Be confident you are doing the will of God, and make sure you and your mate are in harmony and full agreement concerning your final decision—especially if it involves a third party.

Headed for a Miracle

If you choose any one of the alternatives in this chapter just because they are available, you may be robbing yourselves of a great blessing. The best solution to your infertility problem may be one you have overlooked.

I know many couples whose reproductive systems have been miraculously healed by God, enabling them to conceive and bear children. Their faith and confidence in the Lord Jesus Christ has increased as a result. God will give you the desire of your heart if you trust in Him and do not fret and do not look to evil. (See Psalm 37.) Do not exclude the possibility of miraculous intervention by God to alter a physical condition.

A miracle is God interrupting the normal order of things to immediately bring a change through His power to accomplish His will. My wife and I have experienced many healings personally. As a pastor, I preach about the miraculous power of God and pray for people to be healed.

During the twelve years of our ministry, Rebecca and I have observed scores of scriptural healings, including many with fertility complications. We have prayed for people who have been supernaturally touched by God. A miracle is a viable alternative to infertility.

There are several examples in the Bible of women who were unable to conceive until God intervened. Reading the stories of Sarah, Rachel, Hannah, and Elisabeth will increase your faith and encourage you to seek God's will in this area of physical healing.

Becky and I have many friends who, while battling infertility, were touched during a healing service and soon after conceived a child. They had even received a word from God beforehand that this was going to happen.

With great anticipation, Becky and I began to attend as many healing and miracle rallies as possible. One night, the speaker proclaimed that God was healing infertility problems. We, along with another couple, stood up to claim our healing. The other couple conceived weeks later and eventually had a beautiful baby.

If God is going to heal you, He will make that clear to you in your own spirit through His personal word to you. Well-meaning Christian brothers and sisters may tell you that God has told *them* that you are going to have a baby, but they sometimes mistake their own personal desire for you as the will of God. When pregnancy doesn't happen, then you feel condemned or become angry with God. Spiritual discernment is absolutely necessary in this very delicate area.

In spite of our disappointment, Rebecca and I didn't give up. We marched from rally to rally to make sure we didn't miss God's timing. It's funny how we think His timing is related to a specific circumstance or experience.

After every rally, I would go back to my doctor so he could be amazed at the tremendous healing. I told him God was going to heal me. But to this day, when passing him on the street, he still looks at me with a puzzled, annoyed expression on his face. When we act in presumption, we create confusion in others and keep God from doing the real work of healing that He wants to do.

At the time, Rebecca and I were headed for a miracle, but not the kind we expected. God had a plan for our lives that would be life-transforming. But we had to learn that we cannot reduce God's perfect plan to our limited human perspective.

If physical healing had come at that point, it would not have been spiritually healthy for me. I was not yet ready for the great things God was about to do. He knew His time schedule, and the Bible says, "He has made everything beautiful in its time" (Ecclesiastes 3:11).

CHAPTER SIX

We Have a Problem

Rebecca and I had considered each of the available options and ruled them all out: some of the medical alternatives were unscriptural and humanistic; expensive experimental surgery was unreliable; adoption seemed too costly to consider.

We were left feeling empty-handed and depressed, with no place to turn. Searching for consolation and guidance from a Christian perspective proved to be a futile effort. At the time, valuable information about infertility and how to deal with it was almost non-existent. We could find no clear answers to guide us through our maze of distortions. As with any emotionally draining problem, the possibility of injury or defeat was high.

Infertility was an extremely private and delicate matter—especially for me. Instead of dealing with the problem up front, I put it on the proverbial back-burner to simmer. But it didn't go away; it only got hotter and hotter. Our marriage took serious blows while I postponed any effort to resolve the hurt.

We all know of people who have died from cancer because they refused to admit they actually had the dreaded disease. Infertility may not be a life-threatening condition, but marriage, self-identity, and intimacy with God have a high mortality rate among infertile couples. The enemy wages war in these areas, launching an attack on the spiritual and marital life of the husband and wife.

One day when I came home, I found Rebecca sobbing uncontrollably on the bed. With pre-menstrual syndrome and the beginning of cramps, her emotions were at their peak. Everything about this time of the month reminded her that our home was absent of children.

As I watched helplessly, God spoke to me and said, "It's time for *you* to be honest with your feelings." I remained in silence most of that evening trying to accept the reality of the situation. This time there was no way to talk myself out of the dilemma. Our infertility loomed before me in panoramic color.

I finally had to admit to myself and to God, "We will never have children of our own."

An Angry Reaction

The pounding facts dominated my waking hours. With no possibility of ever having children, we felt God had failed us in our most important need. How could He be relied upon in other matters when He would not resolve so simple a problem as this?

Resentment and anger enveloped my whole life, limiting what God could do through me. An attitude change was vital to any hope of accomplishing His purpose in Rebecca and myself.

My lack of trust in God's ways was on the verge of polluting my whole life. I had a bad attitude. Although I accepted my present infertility, I did so with disdain.

"Repent of your attitude" was the message that kept coming to me day after day as we prayed about the next step to take. Repent? I didn't ask for infertility. I didn't go get a vasectomy to terminate reproductive possibilities. Although I was questioning God, my questions didn't bother Him as much as my attitude did.

My reaction to the situation was one of sarcastic anger. "God, if You created me, then there are some defective parts." Amazing how we try to evaluate divine operations with human logic. Yet, God always interrupted my reasonings with, "My ways are higher than your ways."

Anger in itself is not wrong, but Scripture does give a word of caution: "In your anger do not sin" (Ephesians 4:26). Complications arise when anger is uncontrolled or directed at the wrong source. It's not a question of anger being present but rather what we do with anger and how is it ultimately resolved.

Anger can be a significant factor in the healing process. In fact, healing may be delayed until anger toward infertility is expressed. I felt cheated, ripped off, and violated. Until I was able to acknowledge my feelings and direct my anger at the right source, complete healing evaded me.

Anger is most serious and damaging when it is directed toward God. But it's easy to blame Him. After all, isn't God in control of everything that happens to us? Besides, only He is powerful enough to reverse the malfunction. Doctors can attempt it with some possibility of success, but God can do *anything*—if He wants to. The issue becomes one of God's sovereignty. Why won't He change things for my best?

God was sovereign, but I thought He had made a mistake in this case and needed to change His mind. I decided to implement the "Moses Alternative." Moses had beseeched God to reverse His decision to destroy the rebellious Israelites in the desert. God changed His mind then, and I could make Him do it again.

It wasn't that God *couldn't* change the circumstances, but rather that He wanted us to demonstrate our trust in Him.

Trusting God means relying upon His divine order when circumstances for the moment appear to be favoring our failure not our success.

That truth was too cloudy to see then. Instead, I was headed for a collision with my own pride.

A Flaw in the System

I knew the Bible verse that says we are to express trust in God's order by being thankful—whatever the circumstances and in spite of our feelings: "Give thanks in all circumstances, for this is God's will for you in Christ Jesus" (1 Thessalonians 5:18). Such an approach was clearly out of the question. Thanking God for something I was absolutely opposed to seemed ridiculous.

My greatest concern was *my* faithfulness to God and *His* apparent unwillingness to reward such a marvelous example of service and commitment. We had only one request: to bear and raise children. Was that too hard for God? No expressions of appreciation would come from my heart until this issue was fully resolved!

The bitterness that had gripped my heart was created by a wound deeper than the infertility. There was a flaw in my whole belief system. This unique crisis only uncovered the problem that had always been a part of my life: I felt God owed me something, and I was ever waiting to collect on my bounty.

Imagine what a dangerous spiritual tightrope I was walking. I shudder to think what might have happened if God had not brought me to my senses. Scripture tells us that ideas that exalt themselves against the knowledge of God will weaken our spiritual potency. (See 2 Corinthians 10:4,5.) Not only that, but a wrong thought can blossom into sin. (See James 1:13-15.)

Although the Lord repeatedly provided opportunities for me to obey His Word and get on the road to recovery, I refused to respond and remained for a while in a state of rebellious ingratitude. Now I can understand why our heavenly Father insists on a steady diet of the Bible in our lives. It allows Him the liberty to combat painful and dangerous tendencies with the power of His Word.

Gently but firmly, the Lord began to show me that I had forgotten His promise: " 'For I know the plans I have for you,' declares the Lord, 'plans to prosper you and not to harm you, plans to give you hope and a future' " (Jeremiah 29:11).

I remembered the story of Joseph. (See Genesis 37-45.) He was trapped and forgotten in prison. Yet, the entire nation of Israel was saved from starvation because Joseph was in the right place at the right time. So great was the end result that Joseph could look back on his years of detainment without bitterness. There were negative circumstances in his life, but he overcame them.

One day the inner voice of the Holy Spirit spoke to my heart and said, "I purchased your life at Calvary." As I pondered those words, the reality that I belonged to God began to sink in. My perspective changed, and I saw that He could only do what is best for me. If His plan for my life is perfect, how could I continue to be bitter toward Him and my circumstance?

Following the Holy Spirit's careful workings in my life, I asked God's forgiveness for not trusting His ways and for questioning His motives. It was then that healing began.

A New Oneness

The day that Rebecca wept uncontrollably over the hopelessness of our situation was a day of new beginnings for us. Suddenly I discovered a new oneness with my wife. We had known the usual experiences equated with oneness in marriage—planning, dreaming, growing, and ministering together. Now we were one in uncontrollable grief—the pain of loss and failure.

As I allowed myself to completely hurt, the facts and feelings lying dormant in my heart finally reached the surface. Grief made me painfully aware of my own inadequacy, leaving me helplessly crying out to the Father.

Tears bring healing; no wonder God made us with tear ducts. They are the physical outlet for our dammed up emotions. In the Psalms, David demonstrated the ability to weep, "The Lord has heard my weeping" (Psalm 6:8). I was learning that the tears of grief could wash away the anger, resentment, and depression.

Whenever we experience grief, we need to go ahead and cry. If we allow ourselves to feel the pain and express our emotions, grief will pass much sooner. The worst thing we can do is to ignore or bury our true feelings. Grief is unavoidable and normal. You can't go around it. The only way to deal with grief is to *walk through it.*

There is a danger involved in grieving—you can get locked into it and never come out. Some people live their whole lives feeling sorry for themselves. We need to accept the grief period, allow ourselves to heal during it, and then release it to the Lord.

It was a painful walk for Rebecca and me, but at last we were moving together hand in hand. We had finally aligned our spirits on this issue, and we were *one* in our pain. God's Word says the authentic proof of being one is the ability to suffer and rejoice together. (See Galatians 6:2 and Romans 12:15.)

When my wife was down and depressed, I made myself strong so I could help her. Rebecca did the same for me.

We would remind one another that things will get better and tomorrow will be brighter.

During this grief period, the infertile couple should help one another look at life in a positive way. Plan things you have always wanted to do. Tackle projects around the house, take up a new sport, or become active in church and community activities. Keep yourselves busy.

Rebecca and I had always wanted to go to Hawaii, so we planned a trip during this time and had a fantastic time. Schedule a vacation, complete that unfinished degree, or develop a skill or talent that has been lying dormant. By setting new goals, your thoughts are not concentrated on your grief, and complete healing becomes only a matter of time.

Our Infertility

From early childhood little girls play with baby dolls and lavish their affection on them. It's natural and beautiful. Motherhood is one of those instincts that a woman feels compelled to fulfill.

Denying a woman any hope of having a baby of her own brings tremendous hardship on her. Scripture reveals the sufferings of women who, for many years, were unable to have children: Sarah, Rachel, Hannah, and Elisabeth. Childbearing has a direct effect on a woman's worth and value as a person.

Just when I thought we had dealt with the worst of our pain, another festering wound surfaced. During a disagreement in our bedroom, a comment was made that brought Rebecca's feelings out into the open. We had disagreed mildly on a subject so insignificant that neither of us can recall it.

In the course of this skirmish she blurted out, "It's because of *you* that we can't have babies!"

As soon as she realized what she said, Rebecca wept bitterly. My mild, tender wife who would lay her life down for anyone had a deep hurt. One of her basic functions as a woman and her existence as a person was in question. A subject of no great importance brought the wound to the surface.

Her words penetrated me like a laser beam. Instead of standing together to fight against the infertility, we faced each other like two boxers ready to exchange blows.

We were both acquainted with other couples who had divorced because of this problem. The enemy likes to use infertility as a wedge to destroy a God-ordained relationship. Responding rightly, however, can create a marriage capable of defeating any opposition. If we could rise above this, I told myself, imagine the faith and strength that would be planted in our marriage. God must have powerful plans for the Larsons.

After that awful scene in the bedroom, Rebecca and I decided to face this dilemma together. We committed ourselves to not viewing infertility as just *my* problem. In fact, it was my wife who suggested that we see it as *our* problem. She reminded us that the vows we exchanged in the late 70s declare "for better or for worse."

Rebecca and I started saying, "This is *our* infertility problem." We would ask each other, "What are *our* alternatives?"; "What is God saying to *us* in this matter?"

Infertility is not one marriage partner's problem; it belongs to both. We should never even entertain the thought of getting another partner just because our present one cannot give us what we most desire—a child. You are married to the one God wants for you, and to divorce over infertility is wrong. First of all, it is unscriptural; secondly, it would be for a selfish reason.

Working Together for Good

God's Word teaches that a husband and wife become one flesh. (See Genesis 2:24 and Matthew 19:5.) When a need arises in one partner in this covenant relationship, both partners are affected. Satan would like to use this need to divide and conquer, but the Holy Spirit can use it to bind you together as never before.

You can make this a time of positive growth in your marriage, but it will require care and concern on the part of both husband and wife. When dealing with our mates, we must be careful not to make any unnecessary demands upon them. Encouragement and praise will help your mate overcome any feelings of inferiority and inadequacy. Never say anything that will hurt your partner, even in jest or in the presence of others.

Touching, kissing, caressing, holding hands, and other physical expressions are very important during this period of adjustment and challenge. We will discuss the particular problems surrounding the sexual relationship in the next chapter.

This season of "just the two of you" is a great opportunity to spend quality time together. When you do become parents, finding time to be alone together is much more difficult. You will always have to locate a babysitter and arrange for transportation, etc. Do things now that you may not be able to do later.

Rebecca and I decided to write this book together. We wanted to use our infertility to draw us closer—not pull us apart. Infertility affects a couple, and we wanted to share with others how the marriage relationship can be strengthened through this painful experience.

Infertility can draw you and your spouse together like never before. What a wonderful possibility! This potentially disastrous situation can provide greater opportunities for intimacy.

As you draw closer to one another, God will guide you into a most remarkable love relationship—one that other couples will come to admire and respect. Together you can rejoice in God's goodness and plan for your life, and *He* will receive all the glory.

CHAPTER SEVEN

Sex and the Infertile Couple

Infertility had taken the fun out of sex. With semen analysis and temperature charts, the spontaneity was gone. "Come home, Ray, right now!" my wife would call anxiously. Sex had been reduced to a programmed medical procedure, becoming more of a chore than a blessing.

Just weeks before we received the deadly blow to our hopes for a family, Rebecca and I had followed the doctor's advice: "Have relationships daily for one month so that you can be sure not to miss ovulation." Such a marathon is in itself enough to diminish anyone's desire—in spite of what the experts say about daily sex. A normal sex life doesn't follow such a rigorous schedule.

Like clockwork we didn't miss a day. Near the end of the month, Rebecca and I were looking forward to a little break. Oh, it was fun and sometimes hilarious, but enough is enough. We weren't planning to keep up that pace!

Then, just as we were recovering from our month-long marathon, the shock of our infertility hit us. We were one of those rare exceptions to normalcy. The pain injured my masculinity and wounded Rebecca's femininity in a way that became hazardous to the health of our marriage.

Being able to parent a child is a part of the male image. I related infertility to impotency. Masculinity raced away from me before I even knew what was happening. Like a styrofoam cup that had sprung a leak, the desire for sex drained out of my life.

Being with Rebecca was a clear reminder—more like a trumpet blast—proclaiming that I had failed as a man. Failed to be normal! Failed to believe God for a miracle! *Just plain failed!*

Something strong and deep needed to grab our hearts and release us into the true meaning of relationship. Allowing healing to take place in this very significant area of our lives was vital to continued growth in our marriage.

Returning this precious area of husband/wife sharing to normal would require a major change in my thinking. To salvage my ego and our marriage, God would have to break through my preconceived ideas concerning maleness.

I thought about Jesus, John the Baptist, and others who had never fathered children. In fact, they had even given up the right to be married. Yet, their lives reflect the epitome of masculinity. It began to dawn on me that my maleness did not depend on my ability or inability to reproduce my own offspring.

Fulfillment and meaning in life cannot be reduced to one area—especially one that is beyond human ability to correct. The apostle Paul declares that he had "a thorn in the flesh" (2 Corinthians 12:7)—an area of his life or experience that only God could remove and that He chose not to take away. I began to see my problem in a different light than before.

A New Approach

During this time, our sex life did not die; it just became inconsistent and tedious—something it was never intended to be. But where do you turn for answers to such a private and delicate problem?

One seminar professor told a group of us that he counsels infertile couples who have a dead marriage to divorce then start all over. Aside from the obvious stench of worldly thinking, that kind of advice has the odor of total unbelief attached to it. It says that the Holy Spirit is not powerful enough to bring the victory.

Unfortunately, this kind of counsel sometimes finds its way into the church. That's why the apostle John says, "Do not believe every spirit, but test the spirits to see whether they are from God, because many false prophets have gone out into the world" (1 John 4:1). Make sure anyone who counsels you can verify their advice from Scripture.

While facing this dilemma, even well-meaning Christians gave us some ungodly suggestions. One person told us to use pictures to stimulate sexual desire. Of course, we refused to follow such destructive and unwise counsel. Using literature designed for the purpose of producing lustful and wicked thoughts has no place in the bedroom of Christian believers.

When I went to God's Word for help, I discovered that, like praying and talking together, *sex must be regular.* "The husband should fulfill his marital duty to his wife, and likewise the wife to her husband . . . Do not deprive each other except by mutual consent" (1 Corinthians 7:3,5). This command from Scripture launched a new beginning in our marriage.

The need to obey God's Word in the area of sexual responsibility is something I had never before considered. In obedience, I made sure that we had sexual encounters at regular intervals.

Obedience to God's Word is the safeguard to Christian living. This principle works in any area of life. If we do what God's Word says, we will begin to move into the abundant life of Christ. The design is flawless. "His divine power has given us everything we need for life and godliness" (2 Peter 1:3). The Bible is the blueprint for total fulfillment in every area of our lives.

I contacted my dear friend, Dr. Wade Goodall, a trained marriage and family counselor who is also a pastor and dynamic Christian. Wade and his wife were also unable to bear children, so I confided in him about my declining interest in sexual contact with my wife.

He counseled me, saying my reaction was normal. Then, he reminded me that God designed the sexual experience to be one of pleasure, joy, and intimacy between a husband and wife. Sexual expression in marriage is far more than the physical drive the humanists try to make it.

His advice was to approach the sexual experience for the purpose of intimacy, sharing, and pleasure. It wasn't until later that I realized this was life-changing counsel.

The Sex Expert

Rebecca and I had perceived the essence of masculinity and femininity to be the ability to reproduce and bear children. Because we could not fulfill that image, we drew defeating conclusions like, "If we can't produce children, why be sexually involved?"

In our confusion, we decided to go to the Expert: "So God created man in his own image, in the image of God he created him; male and female he created them" (Genesis 1:27). Who knows more about masculinity and femininity than our Creator?

Rebecca and I began to spend time in prayer together like never before. As we sought God's wisdom and stopped leaning on our "own understanding" (Proverbs 3:5), He brought new depth to our limited vision. The Lord not only heard our questions, but He began to change the way we thought about ourselves.

God transformed our self-perceptions by allowing us to see who we are through His purposes. We realized that hearing God's voice and fulfilling His will for our lives was the yardstick He uses in measuring our character.

God's priorities for this time in our lives became clear to us: to love one another with tenderness and to strengthen our marriage with spiritual and physical unity. This simple revelation freed us to be the kind of caring mates to each other we had always desired to be.

As we began to see ourselves the way God sees us, the barriers between us melted away, launching our relationship into a new dimension. Our true masculine and feminine attributes then found unique opportunities for expression that brought us joys we had never experienced before.

Our relationship as husband and wife was no longer plagued by the thought of a childless home. As we began to see one another as that special person God had placed in our lives to be our mate, our intimacy took on new meaning.

Ed Wheat, M.D. and Gaye Wheats' book on the deep meaning of sexuality in marriage titled, *Intended for Pleasure*, greatly helped us. After battling the pains of infertility, we began to take the final step toward recovering that special place sexual relations has in marriage. In fact, the Lord led us toward an even higher value of being together than we had ever believed possible.

As we allowed God to renew our minds and give us His thoughts, a revolutionary view of sex and ourselves came forth. We realized there is a lot more to sexuality than reproduction. God purposed marital relations to be one of the highest forms of communication and joy between a husband and wife.

We knew victory was emerging when the romance fully returned. Rebecca and I began enjoying being together—as two committed to one another for life. The sexual experience became a unique way of expressing our love for one another. In fact, our relationship became more beautiful than in all our previous years of marriage.

CHAPTER EIGHT

Misery or Ministry?

Before the infertility dilemma was resolved in our lives, Rebecca and I found ourselves headed toward the pit of despair. Our growth as Christians was stalemated because of the misery that infertility, and our response to it, had created.

Although we felt no one fully understood what we were going through, we still harbored the hope that someone would help us find a way out of our dilemma. Frantically, we ran from one person to another, looking for someone to minister to our needs. Yet our countenance communicated a desperation that sent friends and family scurrying in the opposite direction. We turned every conversation to the subject of infertility, but most people didn't have the slightest idea how to discuss it—let alone know how to help us.

We were looking for someone to carry our burden. In our misery we had forgotten that God's Word tells us to "carry each other's burdens, and in this way you will fulfill the law of Christ" (Galatians 6:2).

Some of God's principles defy logic and appear opposite to our human perspective on things. But Jesus said, "Whoever finds his life will lose it, and whoever loses his life for my sake will find it" (Matthew 10:39). This truth was like a narrow passageway that eventually led us out of our misery and into ministry. We realized that God wanted us to be reaching out to help others instead of trying to draw in support for ourselves.

Immediately, we thought we should find people who, like ourselves, were infertile. In our common state of emergency, we could minister to them and they could minister to us. There are times when God ordains such an encounter, but we soon discovered it was difficult to help others who were struggling to stay afloat on the same tiny life raft.

During this time, Rebecca and I held the positions of Singles Ministers at our church. With renewed vigor we began pouring our lives into the needs of that particular community. There we found people who were hurting as much as and even more than we were.

Our infertility stopped dominating every conversation and friendship. People began to have a sense of response around us again. Little did we realize that our hearts were being healed as we focused our attention away from ourselves and toward the needs of those who were lonely, depressed, and heartbroken.

Reaching Out to Others

Infertile couples, like anyone else, need to get involved with regular ministry functions that fit God's unique call on our lives. Look for opportunities that are suited to your particular gifts and talents.

The principle of ministering to others provides tremendous healing. It pulls you out of yourself and your private world of pain. That in itself is a major blessing.

Reaching out to others in need allows you to gain a good perspective on your own problem. Certainly, you have a crisis; no doubt you have pain. But there are those in worse circumstances than your own. Childless couples are not unique—everyone has problems.

Soon, you begin to identify with the 1 Corinthians 12 perspective on the Church being a body. When one part hurts, the others hurt with it. Think about this for a minute. What do you do when one part of your physical body hurts? Don't other parts, some far removed from the pain, rally to resolve that hurt? This is also true in the body of Christ. Often, a person unrelated to your particular need or situation can be the most beneficial in helping you through your crisis.

Your misery will spread, however, and decay will set in if you spend all your time nurturing your own wounds. Healing begins to take place when we get into the lives of others and expose our own need to God's light. Those who keep exclusively to themselves have only misery. Those who seek to serve others receive ministry and begin to resolve their own personal pain as well.

History is full of those who, in great need themselves, sought to help others and became heroes of faith. The apostle Paul, with a thorn in the flesh, never let that stop him from accomplishing the great task God set before him. He certainly asked that it be removed, and that is a legitimate request; but he never let it cripple his potential in God.

Filling Up the Holes

No matter where you are in your infertility crisis, don't allow time to waste away. You may still be grieving over your loss, waiting for test results, looking into medical alternatives, or considering adoption. At whatever stage you find yourself—reach out to others!

One childless couple tells how after many long years of pursuing options and alternatives, they soon began to realize their entire life was in misery. They had let their life ebb away while every free moment had been consumed by the pursuit of a solution to their infertility that never did materialize.

Reach out to others, and walk through any door that becomes available to you. Instead of sitting and being consumed with the problem of infertility, look for ways to help others. Soon you will accumulate to yourself much fruitful ministry. Although you do it day by day, and it appears very little at the time, in the long run it will be a major accomplishment. As the years go by, you will begin to see how much God has done through your life.

The cry of our hearts as infertile couples is to have someone understand and give us compassion. But don't expect compassion if you are unwilling to be sensitive to others who are facing hard times or experiencing pain.

Because of our own suffering, Rebecca and I can better understand people who are hurting. While their circumstances may be different from our own, we don't have to fully understand what they are going through to hurt with them. We just have to know what it means to be heartbroken and discouraged.

Many infertile women have found themselves involved in the very unique ministry of reaching out to women who have unwanted pregnancies. Because of embarrassment and the inconvenience of bearing a child, these pregnant women are looking for alternatives. Through a local pro-life group, Rebecca was able to counsel many young women. As a result, she prevented them from making a horrible mistake and saved many babies from being aborted.

Rebecca and other infertile women have taken their own pain and used it to thwart Satan's plan to destroy innocent babies. In addition, they have spared many pregnant women the years of grief and heartache that would have resulted if they had gone through with an abortion.

Husbands can also become involved in ministries that are helping families in crisis. Big Brothers and Youth Guidance provide an opportunity for men to reach out to children and teens who have no father in the home.

The misery that could potentially be ours can be transformed by God's glorious love into a force for good. As we yield ourselves to Him, the Holy Spirit can use us to change negative situations into positive ones. The key is to reach out to people whenever possible. Become an individual who helps fill up the holes in the lives of others. What a powerful possibility.

Making the Most of Every Opportunity

The apostle Paul tells us to make "the most of every opportunity" (Ephesians 5:16). We are all given the same amount of time each day, and we are all held accountable for our effective use of it.

Making full use of every opportunity is essential to our victory in Jesus Christ. What a fantastic blessing you could be to someone else. Serving others will help you realize your potential to affect your world and Christ's kingdom.

The opportunities are endless: visit the sick, send letters and cards to those who are hospitalized, give to those in financial distress, offer hospitality to those who need a friend.

You could support Christian young people as they prepare for college or go into the ministry or leave for the mission field. If you have musical talent, you could use it to direct youth choirs and singing groups. "But I don't have any talents," you say. Anyone can write letters to young men and women who are away in the military or at school. Or, you could minister to those in your church or community who are living away from home by including them in your family holiday celebrations.

Working in the church nursery and Sunday school program can be a tremendous ministry. As pastors of a local church, Rebecca and I know firsthand the importance of committed teachers. Some of our best workers are people who do not have their own children but who pour out their energy and love into the sons and daughters of others. Working with boys and girls in any setting teaches potential parents how to relate to little ones and makes them aware of the needs of children of all ages.

Foster Care

Although I grew up in several foster homes myself, I didn't fully realize the importance of this ministry until Rebecca and I became pastors of our own church. In the past few years, I have been in contact with a whole subculture of children who, because of circumstances or attitudes, have been removed from their natural parents' home.

One of the exciting aspects of our church's ministry is the emphasis we place on foster care. We have group homes that are part of our fellowship and many families who are providing a Christian home environment to one or more foster children. These foster parents often lead these children to Christ, giving them the power to overcome the problems in their lives.

Ruth Lyons, an active member of our church, is greatly involved in foster care. She describes her ministry in her own words:

> Children are special, whether they come naturally, by adoption, or by foster care. To be

entrusted with the raising up of a child is an honorable position. For it is through the raising up of children that a generation goes on and a nation lives.

Many foster children ask: "Why should anyone love me? I'm the reason my folks aren't together. If I had taken better care of my brother, we'd still be a family. If I'd been a good and quiet little girl, daddy wouldn't be in jail for abuse. I don't do anything right. I'm not pretty. I'm stupid. Nobody loves me, not me."

Many of our children feel this way. They come as little broken vessels trying desperately to hold themselves together all by themselves, whether they be eighteen months old or twelve years old.

Some stay for years or a few months or only two days. What can be done in only two days? First, you can take care of their physical needs. You can accept them as they are, imparting to them a sense of self-worth. You can be interested in what they do in your home. You can let them enjoy their childhood while they have it. You can love them.

Maintaining discipline is always a challenge. Children must understand that there are consequences for broken rules. These are explained to each child who comes into our home. Their boundaries are defined, giving them a sense of security that tells them: Someone does care about what I do.

The children who have come to us, and some who have gone back to their homes, are better behaved, more confident, and academically improved than before. They leave our home with a new concern for others and the knowledge that someone does care. Although they still need more help and nurturing, at least their lives have been focused in a positive direction that offers them hope.

We're not alone in this ministry. We have training sessions and workers to help us, but God is our greatest resource.

Do you have room for one more?

I grew up in foster homes. When I became a young teenager, it was difficult to place me into a foster home situation. People were afraid of fifteen-year-olds and the potential problems they often bring. It is true that teenagers can be a tremendous challenge. But who is to say that you cannot be anointed and empowered by God to overcome what most people would call a lost cause? Thank God, somebody took a chance with me.

While waiting for your own children to come, the Holy Spirit can guide you into the areas of ministry that God wants you to be involved in. As you seek God's plan for your life, you will find great opportunities to help others and tremendous victory as you are obedient to the Holy Spirit. Let God lead you out of misery and into ministry.

CHAPTER NINE

Where Have All the Babies Gone?

Rebecca and I will never forget the first time we attended a meeting for prospective parents held by a local adoption agency. It was certainly not what we expected.

As we entered the room where several other couples were seated, an uncomfortable silence greeted us. Their faces expressed a fear and anxiety that could not be hidden behind forced smiles and poised composures. An undercurrent of jealousy pervaded the group, making us feel like intruders invading their domain.

Later we realized why we had felt this way. These childless couples saw us as their competitors in an arena where hopes were high and prizes were few. Our hearts broke, for them and ourselves, to think we might never have the opportunity to adopt an infant.

It was at this point that Rebecca and I discovered there were few if any babies available. We wondered, Where have all the babies gone?

Just fifteen years ago there were more infants to be adopted than families available to take them. Agencies were busy and thriving. An adoptive couple could almost pre-order what they wanted in a child.

Today, the baby boom is over. Birth control is more widely used and available to all women. But efficient family planning has not created the shortage of adoptable children. I wish that were the case.

Abortion is the new form of birth control. Everyday in America alone, over 4,000 babies are aborted—one every twenty-two seconds. Over 44 percent of all unwanted babies from teenage pregnancies are terminated by abortion. Abortion has become a more acceptable solution to an unwanted pregnancy than carrying a child to full term and giving it up to a loving family to adopt.

Unwed Mothers

Another significant factor has limited the number of adoptable children. The attitude toward unwed mothers and their children has changed. Society has accepted free sex and the pregnancies that result. More and more young women are keeping their babies and raising them alone.

Single parenting is in vogue not only because of divorce but also as a result of pregnancies outside of wedlock. The media portrays single parenthood as an attractive alternative to normal family living. It is true that some circumstances force a parent to raise a child alone, but God's design is for children to be raised by a father and mother who are united in marriage.

The average American teenager (14-17 years old) is not emotionally prepared to handle the enormous responsibilities involved in caring for a child. Yet, nine out of ten teenage girls who give birth decide to keep their babies.

At the time it seems like an exciting thing to do. If they themselves don't feel loved by someone, they think the child will give them the love they are missing. Young, unwed mothers do not realize how this decision locks them and their children into a life of welfare dependency or poverty level income. The dream fades quickly with the reality of dirty diapers, sleepless nights, no time to go out, and very little financial support. Plans for a job, college, and the future have to be put on hold.

The heavy responsibility of raising and supporting a child alone often results in an early marriage of convenience that ends in divorce. This is usually followed by another marriage of convenience, resulting in an unstable and often tumultuous homelife.

The highest levels of child abuse and neglect are among teenage parents. Many times, as the child grows older, the single mother cannot cope and the child ends up being placed in foster homes or made available for adoption at a later age.

On the other hand, some girls are able to keep their babies and go on to rich and rewarding lives. This is especially true of Christian women who have considered all the consequences and are fortunate enough to have loving, supportive parents to stand with them.

We need to pray for this generation of young people—that God will intervene in their lives and bring revival to our nation. Pray that girls with unwanted pregnancies will receive the counsel they need to make the right decision concerning their unborn child.

Where Had We Been?

When Rebecca and I were faced with the facts, we began to wonder where we had been for the past twenty years. We thought adoption was going to be so easy.

Where were we when they legalized abortion in 1973? As college students we had been caught up in our own goals and plans, not realizing that one Supreme Court decision would someday affect the destiny of our lives.

Before Rebecca and I faced infertility, we lived life assuming someday we would have children of our own. We never considered the issue of abortion with great earnestness. Yes, we were Christians. Yes, we knew it was wrong, but we never looked into the alarming facts concerning this issue.

When we finally had to deal with the question, *Where have all the babies gone?* we were forced into awareness. It was hard to believe we lived in a society where any unborn baby who was not wanted could be killed by the mother. What about all the couples who *wanted* that baby?

"Why don't people do something about it?" we cried out to God. The pain suffered by all those dying babies took our attention away from our own personal need. We became literally obsessed with finding a solution to this horrendous problem. It seemed God was saying, "Stop the killing of the innocent!"

Rebecca obtained every available book, periodical, and pamphlet on abortion. For weeks we contemplated the devastating reality of the consequences of this terrible sin against God and humanity. Finally, we began to ask, "Lord, what do You want us to do?"

The subject of abortion makes most of us feel uncomfortable. Our first reaction is to ignore the issues, hoping they will go away or that someone else will fight the battle. When confronted with the facts, many Christians will walk away. Some refuse to watch the films that reveal the horror and painful reality of this procedure. Yet, abortion goes on because of this uninvolved mentality. Our silence condones it.

As Christians, it is our responsibility to know as much as possible so we can combat the wrong perceptions and false ideas that people have about abortion and its consequences.

Rights of the Unborn

Our society has changed. We have become a selfish generation who says, "What can I do for me? My rights come first."

What about the rights of the unborn child? The courts say that a child in the womb is a fetus and not a human being, therefore he or she has no rights. What they are really saying is that the unborn child can't voice his or her rights and opinions.

In a local hospital, a physician aborts a woman's nine month old "fetus" without any fear of legal action being taken or public sentiment being aroused. Down the hall in the same hospital, another doctor feverishly trys to save a six-month premature infant because he fears the parents may sue him for malpractice.

And we cry, Where is justice? Whose rights are being violated?

For those of us who believe, as the Bible teaches, that life begins at conception, we say every child in the mother's womb has a right to be born. Even the defective child deserves a chance to come into the world.

What would you recommend in this case?

> The father has syphilis, and the mother has tuberculosis. They have four children. The first child was blind, the second one died, the third one was deaf and dumb, and the fourth one had tuberculosis. The mother is now pregnant with her fifth child, but is willing to have an abortion if you determine she should. What would you decide for her? If you choose abortion, congratulations, you've just murdered Beethoven.
> *(Medical History obtained from R. C. Agnew, U.S.C. Medical School.)*

The major excuse people use to justify abortions today is that unwanted babies will be a burden to our society. Actually, the real burden on society is the cost of state and federally funded abortions. There is no such thing as an unwanted child—just misplaced children. Hundreds of couples would be willing to adopt that one aborted baby.

Most girls do not know to what extent their children are really wanted. Studies show that unwanted babies who are adopted bring great joy to their new parents and grow up to be successful and well-adjusted people.

Psychological studies have shown that there is no correlation between how a mother feels about a pregnancy at the beginning and how she will feel about her baby after birth. Even women who wanted their children admit there were times that they regretted being pregnant. Any book on pregnancy will tell you that a women's emotions are extremely vulnerable during this time. That's why it is so important for a young, unwed, pregnant woman to receive wise and godly counsel regarding this very crucial and potentially fatal decision.

Who's Killing the Babies?

The Center for Disease Control in Atlanta reports that approximately one out of eight American women have already had at least one legal abortion.

Of the women having abortions, 75 percent are unmarried, 32 percent are teenagers, and 20 percent are repeat customers. In most American cities a teenager may request permission from school authorities to take time off during school hours to get an abortion without parental consent.

Physicians perform 1.2 million abortions per year in the United States alone. That is one abortion for every 2.8 live births. In addition to being a convenience to the immoral and a solution to the perverted, abortion has become a moneymaking scheme for doctors and clinics looking for a fast dollar.

I'm not just talking about the operators of the assembly-line clinics in the low-rent districts of America's big cities. You'd be surprised how many established suburban gynecologists with outstanding reputations are performing abortions.

A pastor's wife we knew went to her doctor for a pregnancy test. When told that the test was positive, she was stunned and said, "Oh, no!" Because of her response, the physician thought she didn't want another baby and immediately suggested an abortion. Her answer was a firm, "No way!"

I hope she went on to tell him that she no longer needed the services of a physician who has so little respect for human life. Before any Christian woman submits herself to the care of a physician or infertility specialist, the first question she should ask is, "Do you perform abortions?"

One doctor who felt he was performing abortions as a *favor* for some of his special clients, was forced to morally deal with the issue when one of his patients asked him about this practice. The patient said that as a Christian she could not continue to see an obstetrician who violated God's laws. Her boldness brought conviction to this doctor's heart, and from that point on, he never performed another abortion.

Women in Distress

The abortion on demand mentality grips many of the clinics and physicians' offices of America. They immediately suggest abortion not as a possible option but as the *only* alternative. And why not? There's a lot of money to be made from the government funding available for performing this procedure.

A nurse, who for several years assisted doctors in performing abortions, now crusades against this terrible holocaust. She knows firsthand the pain that the baby suffers and the agony that the women experience after the procedure.

Her recommendation for stopping the killing is simple: Make all abortions free. Without the enticement of payment, most doctors would stop recommending and performing abortions immediately. All their excuses about "aiding a woman in distress" would suddenly be reversed.

A study and case history of 65,000 women in New York and Hawaii, financed by the National Institute of Health and conducted in part by New York State Health Department, compared the experiences of women who did and did not have abortions. They found that women who had had abortions experienced miscarriages at a 35 percent higher rate than those who had not had pregnancies terminated. They also found other pregnancy problems, including low birth weight and premature birth, to be 25-50 percent higher for women who had had abortions.

But those are facts the doctors and nurses at the abortion clinics never tell a young woman. Here's another statistic they like to keep hidden: in 1977, 68 percent of 104 *patient* deaths, during a second trimester abortion, resulted from physician error. Do you think a doctor who can rip apart and grind up tiny legs and arms cares what happens to the grown woman lying on the table?

Many women suffer physical, emotional, and spiritual trauma for years following an abortion. But you'll never hear that on the evening news or read about it in a woman's magazine.

Life and Death Decisions

We have friends who became aware of a handicapped, retarded teenage girl who was repeatedly raped by a gang.

The physician recommended abortion, but the would-be grandmother of the unborn child was against it. She located a family and asked them if they would be willing to adopt this child when born. They agreed to do so because they believed in the right to life for children.

What happened to the baby who was conceived as a result of this rape of a retarded teenager? She was born perfectly normal with beautiful features. This lovely baby has great potential for the future and has brought tremendous joy to this family.

What would have happened if the physician had had his way? This precious little baby would have suffered the agonizing pain of being destroyed in her mother's womb. Her life would have been terminated, and the adoptive parents would have been robbed of a beautiful child. Many couples will adopt babies regardless of the circumstances surrounding their conception.

Who has the right to determine the quality of the child being formed in the womb? Only God can make that judgment, and we as human beings have no right to decide who is going to live and who is going to die. A tragic circumstance is not made better by allowing something worse to happen. Two wrongs do not make a right.

Ethel Waters, the highly respected singer, frequently shared her testimony at Billy Graham Crusades and sang her favorite hymn, "His Eye is on the Sparrow". This wonderful woman, who came into the world as the result of the rape of her thirteen-year-old mother, stands as proof of God's power to use a life—in spite of its origin.

The story mentioned above is a rare exception. Due to the trauma involved, rape seldom results in pregnancy, especially if the girl goes immediately to the hospital. Mary Schott Ward, coordinator of the National Organization for Women's Committee on Rape, agrees: "As pro-lifers contend, pregnancy resulting from rape is very rare." In a Buffalo, New York study, there has not been a confirmed pregnancy due to rape in over thirty years.

Lame Excuses

Many people argue that abortion is necessary in order to save the mother's life. These are called therapeutic abortions, and the need for them is rare. Only three percent of all abortions are therapeutic in nature. That includes rape, incest, and the life of a mother.

Prenatal care for expectant mothers has progressed to the degree that treatment for most medical problems is possible while the woman is pregnant. New techniques like amniocentesis and sonograms detect early disorders. Sometimes, however, if the baby in the womb is found to be less than perfect, the physician may recommend abortion instead of treatment.

Non-therapeutic abortions have become the second most common procedure after circumcision. These are not performed to insure the life or health of the woman, but rather to insure her absence of distress and her so-called happiness. Ninety percent of abortions done are for convenience and economic reasons. In most cases, selfishness is the number one motive.

Some people think that abortion is justified because unwanted children usually end up battered and abused later in life. Yet this is a totally false notion, says Dr. Edward Lenoski, Professor of Pediatrics at U.S.C. In a recent study of 674 battered children, they found that 91 percent of these children were planned pregnancies—wanted not unwanted children. Only 10 percent were illegitimate.

Statistics also show that since the legalization of abortion, child abuse has risen very sharply along with illegitimate births. Since 1973 child abuse has nearly tripled in the United States. When the Supreme Court devalued the life of the unborn child, it put the health and welfare of many older children at risk as well.

Abortions in the United States alone have killed 9,000,000 children since 1973. The fact is: Abortion is the ultimate child abuse.

Most pro-choice and feminist groups argue that the woman has a right to do what she pleases with her body. They say that government funding for abortions is necessary so that all women— both rich and poor—will be able to exercise their feminine right to be pregnant or not. Using the constitutional right to privacy, they argue that the government should not be able to prevent them from making this choice.

Our laws allow police to enter the privacy of people's homes to stop them from abusing their children. But that same law guarantees the privacy and right of parents to murder their babies before birth.

In fact, aren't many crimes—rape, murder, kidnapping, theft—committed in private because the offender does not want his act to be discovered? Does this mean we should turn our heads the other way so as not to invade others' right to privacy? Of course not! Abortion is murder and cannot be tolerated whether it's performed behind the closed door of a doctor's office or on a street corner.

According to C. Everett Coop, M.D., United States Surgeon General, the excuses that people use for abortions are seldom justified.

God's Mandate to You

We did not introduce the subject of abortion to make you feel guilty or to compel you to do things the Spirit of God doesn't prompt you to do. We do, however, want to indicate some steps you can take to help overcome this tragic holocaust that plagues our nation. Begin to ask the Lord what He wants you to do.

In Appendix I, we have compiled a list of ways you can help. Also included is a list of books and materials you can obtain and research. These will help you understand abortion and gain God's heart on this matter.

The Christian's response to abortion should be three-fold—concern for the baby, the mother, and our society. A great moving of God's spirit on the hearts of people to serve Jesus Christ and to live by His Word would bring an end to abortion. Yet, while we pray for revival, we must make use of every opportunity to stop the killing of innocent babies.

American abortion has been called the Great Holocaust. The 1973 Supreme Court decision to accept legalized abortion for other than dangerous medical reasons can be likened to the 1857 Supreme Court decision declaring that a slave is not a person. Only after years of oppression did the thirteenth and fourteenth amendments to the constitution correct the horrendous practice of slavery. Today, we need an amendment that would declare a child in the womb a living human being.

I am reminded of the passage in Genesis 4 where Cain slays Abel. Cain tries to hide his sin from God, but God says, "Don't you know that your brother's blood is crying out from the ground to me?" Today, the blood of millions of babies is crying out to God.

The Living Bible gives us this mandate: "Rescue those who are unjustly sentenced to death; don't stand back and let them die. Don't try to disclaim responsibility by saying you didn't know about it" (Proverbs 24:11, TLB).

"If you say, 'But we knew nothing about this,' does not he who weighs the heart perceive it? Does not he who guards your life know it? Will he not repay each person according to what he has done?" (Proverbs 24:12). Can this mean us? Let's not keep making excuses for ourselves. Let's get involved in saving the lives of the innocent or we may have to answer to God for standing back and allowing them die.

As Christians, we need to heighten our awareness of the horrors of abortion and overcome it by doing everything we can to stop the holocaust. Let's give these innocent babies, regardless of how they were conceived, the right to live, enjoy life, and be a blessing to others. Most of all let's give them the opportunity to hear the message of the gospel of Jesus Christ and to serve Him and His kingdom.

When Is a Baby Not a Baby?

The fact that the word "abortion" does not appear in the Bible does not mean God is silent on the subject. Rather, we must probe the Scriptures more deeply and in broader context to discern His will on this matter. The word "cigarette" is not mentioned in the Bible either, but it is not difficult for Christians to determine that smoking is harmful.

The basic question we must ask is whether God considers an unborn baby growing in the mother's womb to be a living person. If the answer is "no," then perhaps it's all right to dispose of a fetus as an unwanted appendix or tumor. If the answer is "yes," then we must treat the unborn with all the love and concern due any human being.

The psalmist David tells us that God knew him before he was born:

> For you created my inmost being; you knit me together in my mother's womb . . . My frame was

not hidden from you when I was made in the secret place . . . Your eyes saw my unformed body. All the days ordained for me were written in your book before one of them came to be (Psalm 139:13-16).

This passage makes it clear that human life begins at conception.

God spoke to the prophet Jeremiah and said, "Before I formed you in the womb I knew you, before you were born I set you apart" (Jeremiah 1:5).

In Luke chapter one, Scripture calls the entity in the womb a *baby*: "When Elizabeth heard Mary's greeting, the baby leaped in her womb, and Elizabeth was filled with the Holy Spirit. In a loud voice she exclaimed: 'Blessed are you among women, and blessed is the child you will bear!' " (verses 41,42).

The Greek word for baby in the womb (brephos) is also used to denote a baby after birth in Luke 2:12-16; an infant in Luke 18:15; and a child in 2 Timothy 3:15. In these passages, no distinction is made between born and unborn children.

When the angel appeared to Zechariah (the father of John the Baptist), he said the child to be born "shall be filled with the Holy Ghost, even from his mother's womb" (Luke 1:15, KJV). How can an unborn baby be filled with the Holy Spirit of God unless he or she is a living being?

The personalities of unborn children are already formed before birth. When Rebekah was pregnant with the twin boys, Jacob and Esau, "the babies jostled each other within her, and she said, 'Why is this happening to me?'. . . The Lord said to her, 'Two nations are in your womb, and two peoples from within you will be separated; one people will be stronger than the other, and the older will serve the younger' " (Genesis 25:22,23).

The apostle Paul writes that God "set me apart even from my mother's womb, and called me through His grace" (Galatians 1:15, NASB).

Clearly, these instances from Scripture show that the unborn is a person. You may be thinking that these are special cases. But let's consider the most unique person of all, our Savior Jesus Christ.

Scriptures tell us that in His human form Jesus was like us in every way. (See Hebrews 2:17.) From the moment of conception to the day He died on the cross, He lived in humanness like you and me. Yet, there is no question of Jesus' personhood before birth: "In the beginning was the Word, and the Word was with God and the Word was God. . . . And the Word became flesh and made his dwelling among us" (John 1:1,14).

By taking on the form of man, the Son of God has given us as human beings inestimable value. No exception can be made because of our size or shape or where we reside. From the moment of conception, we are indeed precious in God's sight.

The Bible is the source of all truth. For greater understanding about this issue of abortion, research the following scriptures and ask the Holy Spirit to open your heart to God's perspective on life and death.

Where do the unborn come from?

Genesis 1:1,27	Genesis 33:5
Job 10:12	Genesis 25:21
Psalm 127:3	

How does God feel about the killing of innocent babies?

2 Kings 17:16-20	Leviticus 20:1-5
Jeremiah 32:35	Amos 1:13
Jeremiah 7:6; 22:3,17	Exodus 23:7

Proverbs 6:16-17   Genesis 9:6
Exodus 20:13   Matthew 5:19

Does a woman have a right to her own body?

1 Corinthians 6:19,20

What does God say to those facing a crisis situation or a physical problem in their lives?

Isaiah 45:9,10   2 Corinthians 12:7-9
1 Corinthians 10:13   Ephesians 5:20

What does God say to the woman who has had an abortion?

1 John 1:9   Romans 6:1,2
Galatians 6:1.

What does Jesus expect of His Church?

Matthew 22:36-40   Matthew 25:37-40
1 John 2:4-6   Matthew 5:14

Whose laws should the Christian obey? God's or man's?

Romans 12:2

CHAPTER TEN

All God's Children

If God isn't calling you to be a childfree couple, and a medical solution doesn't seem right or possible for you, another alternative is available—one that is scriptural and has a very high rate of success. Adoption.

Did you ever consider that *all* of God's children are adopted? (See Romans 8:16.) The Creator of the universe, compelled by His love, takes us, lost in sin, and adopts us as His own. "In love, he predestined us to be adopted as his sons through Jesus Christ, in accordance with his pleasure and will" (Ephesians 1:4,5).

Although we do not deserve His love, God calls us by His name and grants us His inheritance. (See Romans 8:17.) Our heavenly Father adopts us as His own and even molds us to take on His character. (See Romans 8:29.)

As God's children who are formed in His image, we, too, are granted the privilege of loving and shaping the lives of those who are not naturally our own. In fact, nothing more clearly demonstrates the character of God than His working within us to make us willing to extend ourselves to be family to a little one—one who neither asked nor is in a natural position to be our child. Adoption is a unique way for us to allow the majestic love of God to flow through us.

God wants to release that love in those of us who cannot bear biological children. As we yield ourselves to adopt and raise children, God can use us to accomplish His plan and purpose in their lives. He can place children in our homes to become "sons and daughters of God" who will bring glory to His name.

Learning Our Lessons

Long before our first child came into our home, God was working in two areas of our lives that were crucial to our receiving the children He had for us.

Our first lesson dealt with contentment. We had to learn to be content with the possibility that we might never have children. At the same time we had to trust God the Father, knowing that He had given us specific promises. A unique tension developed as we learned to keep His promises hidden in our hearts yet not to focus on the fulfillment of them. We learned to be content, to obey Him, and wait for God to open the right doors.

After Rebecca and I yielded our rights to God, we were willing to live the rest of our lives childless—if that was His will for us. It was then that God began to plant in our hearts the need and the desire to adopt children. When God plants that seed, He then provides the child—and the means.

Our second lesson involved thanksgiving. We had to learn to thank God, believing that He was in charge of our spiritual, emotional, and physical lives. The Bible says, "In everything give thanks: for this is the will of God in Christ Jesus concerning you" (1 Thessalonians 5:19, KJV).

In His sovereign plan, our loving heavenly Father had taken care of everything. As we began to thank God for the specific circumstances in which we found ourselves, He began to wonderfully supply.

God met our every need. Oh, we had to scrimp and save and be frugal with our money. But where we lacked, He supernaturally provided. In the end He gave us a little extra for the special things we wanted to give to our children. We found God to be faithful at every step along the way.

The Grafting-In Process

I've heard people say, "I could never love someone else's child."

Yet, when God places a child in your home, the Holy Spirit grafts that child into your life in such a beautiful and powerful way that you will forget that someone else gave birth to him or her. You will be knit together so naturally and spiritually that there will be no doubt in your heart that this child is yours.

A gardener can take a branch that originally developed from one tree and graft it into another tree. After the initial cutting and splicing, both the tree and the branch must adjust to this new arrangement. The grafting in process takes time, but the end result is a healthier branch and a more fruitful tree.

In the book of Romans, we read how the Gentiles, not being the people of God, are grafted in and become a part of the kingdom of God. If the Holy Spirit can take sinners like you and me and make us the people of God, He can also take a child and make him or her part of your family.

Some people think that you can't love adopted children the same way you love children to whom you've given birth. I disagree. No one can say to us that our two children are not completely our own. They are very special before the Lord. God has provided them in a miraculous way.

Many people are afraid of adoption and all the complications it involves—legally, emotionally, and spiritually.

How do you raise a child as your own when you must constantly remember that he or she had other origins? Many couples wonder what will happen if their adopted child later wants to look for his roots.

Bill Gothard, founder of *Institute in Basic Youth Conflicts,* has done extensive study on the emotional conflicts that adoptive children and their parents can encounter. He gives several suggestions that are helpful to an adopting couple.

He tells parents to hold their adoptive child in open hands, realizing that *every* child is only entrusted to parents by the Lord. Love is not possessive or jealous, as 1 Corinthians chapter thirteen says.

Those who have their own children soon realize, as Dr. C. M. Ward says, "Children must be lent back to the Lord." Any child, whether born naturally to spirit-filled, Christian parents or the result of a pre-marital union between two unsaved teenagers, must be taught to love and obey God. Parents are the agents God uses to raise His children in the fear and the admonition of the Lord.

Remember, your child belongs to God. As Moses' mother did, so you must also place your child in the river of God and let Him guide and direct his or her destiny.

Some adoptive parents try to live as though the natural parent did not exist, but this often creates more problems than it solves. As the child grows older he will naturally want to know about his past. Bill Gothard says not to dismiss or fear the child's curiosity about the natural parents but to be as open and frank as possible.

As soon as the child is able to understand, you should tell the child that you adopted him or her. Explain how God led the child to your family, how God opened the doors, and how He miraculously answered your prayers. The child needs the reassurance of knowing that it was God's love leading you to adopt him or her. Build the child's self-worth by assuring him that he was specially chosen and that God has a wonderful plan for his life.

Parents should encourage the adopted child to focus on his heavenly Father as his source of security. All parents—both natural and adoptive—are frail and human. Only God, our heavenly Father, can provide both parents and children the emotional security we need for this life.

Giving your child this kind of balanced biblical perspective will enable the Holy Spirit to graft the adopted child into your heart and life. When he or she becomes part of your family and takes on your attitudes and mannerisms, it will be clear to you as parents, and to others, that *the child is yours*.

Acting Like Your Father

God in His infinite love made us His own "while we were still sinners" (Romans 5:8). God's love compelled Him not to strike us down in judgment but to create an alternative to bring us life. "God so loved the world that He gave His one and only Son, that whoever believes in him shall not perish but have eternal life" (John 3:16).

We, as believers, begin to act like our Father when we are able to love those who, in the natural, we are unable to love. Through His Holy Spirit, God places in our hearts the power that enables us to love those whom we would not otherwise choose.

I have several friends who are my closest and most loving compatriots. But based on physical circumstances and natural inclinations, they would never have chosen me and I would have never chosen them as friends. But, by the peculiar, supernatural love of God we have been linked together.

In the same way, God brings children and parents of different origin and circumstance together, grafts us into each other's lives, and makes us one family. Adoption is a beautiful, earthly rendition of a masterpiece painted by our Creator. God takes those who were not of His family and makes them eternal members. We likewise take those who are not of our seed and make them our children.

Making the Decision to Adopt

In the 1960s, there was an abundance of babies who needed homes. Public appeals were made regularly by agencies seeking couples and families willing to adopt.

The adoption scene is different today, as we discussed in the last chapter. Because of the casual acceptance of unmarried motherhood and legalized abortion, there has been a steady decline in adoptable babies. In addition, the number of couples unable to conceive a child is greater, and there simply aren't enough adoptable children to go around.

The question is: How do you climb the mountain of restrictions, red tape, and risks to find an adoptable child? Adopting a child is no task for the faint-hearted. It can be very discouraging, especially for the childless couple who may already feel deeply hurt, confused, left out, and even rejected by God as being "unparentable."

You and your mate must decide together whether or not adoption is for you. If there is any doubt or hesitation by either partner, wait. It is important that you both fully agree that this is the direction God wants you to pursue.

Don't let the fear of growing old and dying alone affect your decision to adopt. Having children means one hundred percent giving and expecting nothing in return. Make sure your intentions are right and your desires are pure. Pray and ask God to change your heart, removing all selfish motives and unrealistic expectations.

Try to be objective about the pressure that family, friends, and the church can place on the childless couple. People always seem to be wondering why you don't have children, and they tend to assume the worst about you. Don't let their opinions and judgments affect your reasons for wanting a child.

There is a myth that a couple without children is missing something—that their lives are just not complete. A marriage is what you make it, and children don't make a marriage— you and your mate do. If you choose to be happy, you will be—with or without children.

On the other hand, you need to make your decision to adopt as soon as possible. Adoption proceedings can take anywhere from one to five years or even longer. When we were faced with the possibility of waiting such a long time, Ray and I were very upset. Yet, God's timetable is different from man's. Since it takes most couples at least two years to get over the emotional distress that is involved with infertility, some waiting time before adopting is good.

You may be one of those couples in whom God has placed the desire to adopt. The reasons may be unexplainable to someone else, but you know in your heart that God has a child somewhere out there for you. We feel God has allowed specific couples to be in a position to adopt certain, special children who come into this world. These childless couples are *chosen by God* to do this.

Children are a gift from God. He gives some by biological birth and others come through adoption. Either way, they are all gifts from God, and "every good and perfect gift is from above, coming down from the Father of the heavenly lights" (James 1:17).

Against All Odds

In the natural, the odds against finding and adopting a child seem overwhelming. But don't throw adoption out as a favorable alternative. God has never been bound by adoption fees and statistics. In fact, He enjoys accomplishing His purposes against the greatest odds. In that way, He receives the greatest glory and deserves all the credit.

God in His infinite wisdom and understanding can provide the right child or children for your home. Remember this phrase: *Where God guides, He provides.* He is able to do great and marvelous things to bring about His plan.

God's love is creative enough to send children our way. His power is great enough to supernaturally overcome the odds against finding a child in this generation. He can choose a child for us, place him or her in our home, and give us the privilege of raising up world changers for Jesus Christ in these last days.

Moses' mother released her infant son into God's loving hands, unaware of the baby's destiny. Today, some mothers, because of undesirable circumstances, release their children, not knowing what is going to happen to them. Yet, God's hand is on them. Many unwanted children end up in Christian homes where they are raised to fulfill the special plan and purpose God has for their lives.

All over the United States, there are Christian couples who, in spite of the odds, were able to adopt children. God made a way where there was no way. One couple recalls their *"wait of faith"*:

> After several years of marriage and a year of infertility testing, my husband and I decided we would look into the adoption process. In my heart, I felt sure the Lord had a baby for us. It was

waiting for the right baby to come into our lives that tested our faith.

During the year after our infertility testing, several possible adoptions came our way, but nothing worked out. Doubts began to come. We wondered if we weren't rich, cute, talented, spiritual or "just plan good enough" to be selected. Through it all, we felt the Lord saying, "Just wait."

One day while I was praying, the Lord impressed upon me to write down what I wanted in an adoption. At first I resisted saying, "Who am I to tell You what I want? You are God and know which baby and circumstances are best for us." Finally, I surrendered and wrote down six brief, simple requests.

Two days later my husband received a call that we had been selected by a birth mother. I inquired, "Are you sure?" My husband responded reassuringly, "Yes! And she wants you to call her!"

This young woman's first words to me that glorious day were, "Praise God! I'm carrying *your* baby!" As I reached to control my racing heart, I responded, "Praise the Lord." Immediately, the peace of God flowed through me.

She went on to say that as she read our introductory letter, the Lord impressed upon her that we were the couple to raise her child. We both knew that this was the Lord's perfect will.

Our daughter was born three months later, healthy and as cute as a button. All six of my requests, or should I say desires, had come true. The moment we held our daughter, all the pain we had felt before her birth was carried away and is now only a memory. The Lord does give us the desires of our hearts.

The Love Factor

What compelled Rebecca and I to adopt children? God's love! As the apostle Paul said, "Christ's love compels us" (2 Corinthians 5:14). Some of you may have a medical solution to your infertility, but, because of what God has worked in your heart, you will adopt children as well. Others, who read this book and have their own natural children, will also choose to adopt. Why? Because the love of God compels them.

Adoption is God's beautiful, majestic way of taking families and children, making them one, and accomplishing the miraculous plan He stored in Jesus Christ before the foundation of the world. "For those God foreknew he predestined to become conformed to the likeness of his Son" (Romans 8:29).

Adoption has become a blessing to us and to many families with whom we share the experience of being adoptive parents. It is a great privilege and a wonderful opportunity. Acting in love and knowing you are staying within the guidelines of God's Word brings an excitement and blessing far beyond what any man-made medical procedure can achieve. Although medical science has done marvelous things to provide other ways of having children, adoption is the clear biblical alternative.

In the next few chapters we are going to be addressing the many issues surrounding adoption and provide you with some practical guidelines. Before moving on, let me suggest that you take time to pray and examine the motivations of your heart. The Lord may ask you to give up the right to children, or you may need to totally release to Him your perspective on the situation. Then, allow God to weave His beautiful plan into the fiber of your life.

Ephesians 3:20 says that God "is able to do immeasurably more than all we ask or imagine." Our loving heavenly Father can lead you down a path of joy and fulfillment that is beyond your ability to plan or reason out. Give back to Him the desire of your heart, and let Him make the way.

CHAPTER ELEVEN

How to Get the Adoption Ball Rolling

When Ray and I first considered adoption, we had no idea where to begin gathering information or how to proceed. It was distressing to find that the little information that *was* available was written from the world's point of view. Their emphasis was on how to "play the adoption game," not on how to let God direct you. We could find nothing from the Christian perspective.

The purpose of this book is to aid Christian couples in making prayerful, informed decisions about their options. Several ways of adopting children are available—all with their own peculiar circumstances and risks.

Agency adoptions involve state and private agencies that have children and infants available for a variety of reasons.

State and local agencies generally handle "special needs" or children who are hard to place because of their race, their age, a handicap, or emotional problems stemming from abuse or neglect.

Private agencies are often church related or a branch of a pro-life organization. They generally handle infants but may also place older children.

Independent adoptions are generally arranged through a personal contact and usually involve a private doctor and/or lawyer.

International or intercountry adoptions involve the placement of foreign children—Asian, Latin American, etc.— and work through established organizations.

Adopting a child is a very expensive undertaking and can cost anywhere from $3,000 to $10,000. If you truly want to adopt and God is leading you, the money will be provided. It may require great personal sacrifice on your part, but you'll never regret having made it.

According to one report, there are about one million couples wanting to adopt a child. The chances of your dream coming true can seem faint indeed. But our God is the God of the impossible, and the final outcome is in His hand! So, press on with faith and courage, and we will try to help you chart your course.

Finding an Adoption Agency

The most common way of adopting a child is through an established agency. In this chapter, we will outline the procedures and requirements involved in working with an agency. We will provide some general guidelines and also look at some specific adoption agencies.

You can start by contacting your own state department of social services and requesting brochures on general adoption information. This is important since the laws differ from state to state. These brochures will provide names, addresses, and requirements of licensed agencies in your state.

The *Adoption Factbook,* available from the National Committee for Adoption, and *The Adoption Resource Book* by Lois Gilman provide lists of recommended agencies in each state. (See *Suggested Reading.*)

All agencies function somewhat differently. Some are public adoption agencies chartered and supported by state governments. These should be listed in your phone book under human or social services. There are also state licensed private agencies who should be listed under "adoption services" in the yellow pages. Independent services run by religious organizations and private groups can also be found under that same listing.

Some cities have no agencies within their jurisdiction. We know of couples who have relocated just to be able to adopt through a particular agency.

In Appendix IV, we have included a list of adoption agencies by state. This will help you locate the ones nearest you since it is usually easier to adopt within your own state. Some agencies deal only with state residents; others work with many states; and some work with any state in the nation. Be warned that adoption between states can often be complicated and requires expert legal assistance.

In addition to obtaining names and addresses, be willing to tell everyone you know about your desire to adopt. In one situation a woman mentioned to her hairdresser that her daughter and son-in-law had been unsuccessfully trying to adopt a baby for some time. The hairdresser happened to know someone who had just found an infant through a small private agency. The contact led to a successful adoption.

Ray and I left no stone unturned. I hunted down the addresses of all of the agencies I could find. When an agency wasn't located in my home state, I wrote to them instead of phoning.

How do you choose the right agency for you? I suggest you call and talk to someone at each agency, praying for discernment as you do. A telephone conversation can sometimes spark a positive or negative reaction in your spirit. Ask them to send you any information they have and a sample application. This will give you an idea of their philosophy, the requirements couples must meet, and the fees involved in their initial adoption procedures.

Waiting Lists

Before actually applying, we suggest you pray diligently about every source, every suggestion, and every agency you hear about. If you sense that the Lord has given you the go-ahead, then apply to every open agency you find. We recommend that couples be put on waiting lists, even if the agencies tell you it may be a five to ten year wait. You can always take your name off the lists, but it isn't so easy to get placed on them.

Many agencies charge application fees of varying amounts that are not refundable. Beware of this before you apply. We sent a lot of money to many agencies only to have them tell us they were sorry, but they didn't have any babies. They also *didn't* refund our money.

Before you send an application fee, check out what regions an agency serves, what kind of babies they have, what the waiting list consists of, and how long a wait is anticipated. If you are not in an agency's district, you will need to have a home study done by someone in county or state government services or through a private agency that serves your area. You usually have to pay their fee for the home study.

The long waiting lists that most agencies have can be discouraging to hopeful couples. As prospective adoptive parents, you can manage to overcome all the obstacles, meet the many requirements, finally be approved, and *then* find out no babies are available for adoption. There are usually many couples already approved and who have been on the waiting list for months, or even years, before you applied.

Working With an Agency

Adoption agencies have many resources and are able to provide pre-adoption counseling and information along with post-adoption support and guidance. No matter how good the intentions and motivations of both parties, adoption is a stressful situation for everyone involved. Feelings run high, expectations are sometimes exaggerated, and anxiety can abound.

Agencies provide a tremendous amount of pre-adoption "matchmaking" with extensive research into the adoptive parents' and the child's family histories. They conduct several interviews, asking questions, questions, and more questions to insure the best possible blend of a child with new parents.

You will fill out many forms, sometimes up to forty pages, including twenty pages of questions probing every aspect of your personal life. You will probably be scrutinized more carefully than at any other time in your whole life.

Most agencies function from the point of view that they exist to find *families for babies*. Agencies generally have a negative opinion of independent adoptions, seeing them as a means of finding *babies for families*. They believe the child's needs should be placed far above the needs of the adoptive parents.

In most states, the birth parents must sign all rights to the child over to the adoption agency. Upon court approval of their relinquishment, which is irrevocable at that point, the agency becomes the "legal guardian" and can then place the child with prospective parents.

This differs from independent adoptions where the birth parents can change their minds right up until the time the final adoption papers are granted by the court.

Agencies feel that independent adoptions lack security for the adoptive parents, adequate counseling for the birth parents, and the assurance of a healthy, loving home for the child. Many parents who have adopted both ways generally agree that if they were to do it over again, they would choose the agency method over the independent.

The security and peace of mind provided by going through an agency, regardless of the trouble and delay, is preferable to coping with the anxiety and risks of an independent adoption. Ray and I agree with this as well.

Some agencies can be very impersonal. Their attitude often comes across as, "Why are you calling us? Don't you know we don't have any babies? Besides we have a five to ten year waiting list." You are finally reduced to a name and an address on a sheet of paper.

We realize not all secular agencies make you feel this way, but Ray and I experienced this kind of treatment several times. Just be prepared, be gracious, and don't wear your feelings on your sleeve.

Most agencies will inform you that you can attend a group meeting with others who are interested in adopting a child. They will describe the services they can provide, warn of the lack of children available, give approximate time periods you can expect to wait, describe the interviews you will have, outline the fees and general requirements, and answer questions.

If you are not intimidated by all of this and are satisfied with what you have heard about the agency, they will allow you to submit an application and set up an appointment with a caseworker. The first meeting with the caseworker will determine whether or not the agency will accept your application.

You need faith and persistence as you set out to take on the adoption agencies. But be of good cheer. If God has spoken to your heart, then press on like Abraham did and you will receive your blessing.

Bethany Christian Services

I'm sure there are many good adoption agencies, but Ray and I can heartily recommend the one we worked with—Bethany Christian Services. This fine organization has offices throughout the nation, and these are listed by state in Appendix IV. Many of the forms and guidelines provided in this book were made available to us by Bethany.

In addition to their adoption service, Bethany counsels and assists pregnant girls. Their Master's House in Modesto, California is a very modern and beautiful home for unwed mothers. Ray and I continue to support this organization with our financial gifts because we feel they provide such an important ministry.

Bethany's adoption service deals strictly with born-again Christians. They screen each set of prospective parents very extensively to make sure they are believers. Even though Ray and I were pastors of a church, they made sure we really knew Christ as our Savior.

We had written to Bethany Christian Services years before, but they responded saying that they didn't serve our particular area. I filed the letter. Then two years later, I got out my files and rewrote letters to different groups asking about the availability of children. To my surprise, Bethany now had an office in our area, so I asked them to send us their information packet.

This packet included a letter explaining the requirements that applicants must meet. Couples applying for infants must fall within a certain age range, have a diagnosed fertility problem, and have two children or less.

We returned the preliminary application along with the nonrefundable processing fee. Below are sample questions taken from Bethany's preliminary application. This will give you an idea of what to expect.

Preliminary Adoptive Application

Please fill in the following requested information:

Husband's name: _____
Birthdate: _____
Wife's name: _____
Birthdate: _____
Address: _____
Telephone number: _____
Date of marriage: _____

Children? _____ Boy/Girl? _____
Age? _____ Biological/Adopted? _____

Church affiliation: _____
Full communicant members? _____
Pastor's name: _____
Church address: _____

Infertility information: _____
What is the nature of your infertility? _____
What medical treatment has occurred? _____
Has your doctor ruled out conception? _____
List all adoption agencies you have contacted:

_____
_____
_____

Have you filed an application with them? _____
Application date: _____

Additional comments/Interest in special-needs child?

_____
_____

The information Bethany sent us contained their printed fee schedule, based on family income. This let us know from the beginning exactly what our cost would be. It seemed like a lot of money at the time, but Ray and I didn't let financial considerations stop us from finding a child. We knew that God would supply. Having a child was more important to us than a new house, car, travel, expensive clothes, or other material things we could buy.

We did not have to pay the entire fee up front, so we had time to save. If we did have problems, we had the assurance that we could pay over a period of time. Bethany is very good about working out a payment plan.

The Initial Interview

After applying to Bethany and being accepted, we began to attend meetings with them to start the home study. We had seemingly endless forms to complete and lots of questions to answer. This was a time-consuming and some-times exhausting process, but so is pregnancy and labor. It is work getting the gift of a child from God—no matter how you look at it!

At the initial meeting with the agency representative, it is best not to be too rigid in your exact preferences for a child—such as wanting only a blond, blue-eyed, baby girl with no medical problems who is less than two months old. I'm not implying that you should be deceptive; just be cautious.

Agencies are looking for flexibility of attitudes in prospective parents. They have dozens of families who would jump at getting the child I described above, so they don't need another one. They want couples who are open to consider-ing a variety of children for adoption. Being too specific in the early meetings can rule you out as a prospect without allowing you to even proceed beyond the initial interview.

This doesn't mean you shouldn't express any preferences at all, but be open and let them know you are willing to pray about your decision. God also wants you to be flexible in your preferences so that the child He already has chosen won't fall outside your preconceived specifications for "our baby."

You may be asked to complete a form similar to the one below:

Check all the possible categories with which you would feel comfortable.

Age range in months: __ 0-3 __ 3-6 __ 6-9 __ 9-12
Age range in years: ___ 1 ___ 2 ___ 3 ___ 4 ___ 5

Sex:
_____ Male only
_____ Female only
_____ Either sex

Number of Children:
_____ 1 Child only
_____ Sibling group of 2
_____ Sibling group of 3
_____ Sibling group of 4 or more

Racial & Ethnic Group:
_____ White   _____ Mixed White/Black
_____ Black   _____ Mixed Oriental/White
_____ Oriental   _____ Mixed Mexican/White
_____ Mexican   _____ American Indian
_____ Mixed American   _____ Other (Specify)
Indian/White

Medical:
____ Mild ongoing medical handicap
____ Correctable medical handicap
____ Extensive medical handicap

Emotional:
____ Child with behavior problems that need to be
worked through.
____ Child with emotional problems who needs
short term therapy.

Intellectual:
____ Slow learner
____ Mildly retarded

Special Comments: _____

The Home Study

A home study is a study of one's home, lifestyle, and medical history that allows the social worker to become better acquainted with the adopting parents. It is not a white-glove inspection of a person's housekeeping methods, as someone told me. Whenever it was time for the social worker to arrive, I would feverishly dust everything in the house one more time.

Don't believe everything you hear. People will warn you that minor details such as the clothes you wear, the condition of your house plants, and the way you speak can all jeopardize the final approval of your home study. Remember you are dealing with professionals who are interviewing prospective parents not candidates for a Mr. and Mrs. America contest.

The home study consists of three parts:

1. Forms to be completed.
2. Interviews between the social worker
   and the prospective parents.
3. The home study report written by
   the social worker.

In Appendix II, I have created a synopsis of the forms and information required by most agencies. Both prospective parents will fill out these forms.

Checking You Out

The caseworker will check your family history, your background and your finances. They will want to see a doctor's report, the results of current physicals for both husband and wife, and an infertility report in most cases. Most agencies will not place infants with couples who do not have an infertility problem.

Your marriage, health, home life, community, employment and work history will be carefully examined. You will also need your marriage certificate, your birth certificates, photographs of both of you, and a sketch of your home. You will need to have TB tests and chest x-rays and be fingerprinted.

You will be asked for references. We suggest getting five references although you may not need that many. Make up multiple copies and have several on hand.

You and your spouse will be interviewed together, and you will be interviewed individually. These can be trying situations, and it is essential that you have *both* spent time in prayer prior to each meeting—even if it takes all night long. If you and your spouse have an inner peace achieved together through prayer, then you can present a "oneness" as you talk with the caseworker.

It is important that both of you have resolved your feelings about infertility and that you have committed the problem to God. I read of a couple who were going through a home study. The caseworker asked the husband (whose wife had been diagnosed as being infertile), "How do you feel about your wife's infertility problem?" This is definitely a valid but loaded question. After a long pause, he answered with flying colors, "My wife doesn't have an infertility problem, we do."

You can try to plan ahead and think of every possible subject that might arise, but invariably you will be faced with a question that you didn't anticipate. That is why you need the peace of the Holy Spirit flowing within your spirit. God is never caught off guard.

The Real Test

After we filled out all the long, tedious papers, completed the home study, and answered every question, then the real test began. We had to *wait*. This word becomes very real to a childless couple.

We were told it would probably take one to two years to adopt, but Bethany didn't really have a set time limit. In their agency, the pregnant woman is allowed to look through profiles and pictures to select the couple she wants.

If the waiting period becomes longer than the agency had originally projected and you have had no contact from them at all, you need to do some checking. Perhaps no birth mother has chosen you, or maybe your application has been shuffled around and lost in the bureaucratic red tape. It does no harm to call the agency and express your concern. But never forget, prayer always accomplishes greater things than you ever could.

During this time of waiting, prayer is your best source of strength and patience. You need the personal stamina and power to daily submit to God a situation over which you have no human control.

Pray about every aspect of the adoption procedure. Seek God's wisdom for those who are handling your case through the agency. Ask the Lord to be with the girl who is carrying your child at this time. Pray for her pregnancy, her delivery, her release of the child, etc. Ask God to prepare your hearts to receive the child and to begin now to work to make you good parents. Present every detail to the Lord for His perfect will to be accomplished.

While we were waiting for a child, I wrote this prayer letter to the Lord:

Dear God,

I know there is a little mother out there somewhere who is going through more than I'll ever know with all her doubts, fears, and anxieties. She is up against hell itself as she makes the decision to give up her child for adoption. She prays, even if she doesn't know how to pray, that her baby will end up with a man and woman who will care for her child.

God, I pray for this little mother and ask You to take care of her. Give her peace and wisdom as she makes her decisions. Protect and provide for her as she bears this child and then gives the child to a good home where he/she will be cared for by a loving family.

I also pray for that little unborn baby in that girl's womb. Please protect him/her. I know in my heart that he/she is coming to us soon. I feel like I have just found out that I am pregnant with a child. I am so excited. I can't wait to hold our little bundle of joy.

I will praise You every day for this coming answered prayer. Thank You, Father, for giving us the desires of our hearts.

Rebecca

When you are finally selected to receive a child, you will continue to be carefully checked by the caseworker to see how you as parents and the child are adjusting. Until the adoption is finalized by the court, which can take several months depending on your state, the agency is still the guardian of the child.

Once the adoption process is completed and the adoption is finalized, the child becomes legally yours. The waiting is over, and it's time for celebrating and praising God!

As we walked quietly into the house, an awkward silence surrounded us. We nervously sat waiting for what seemed like an eternity. Then this beautiful girl walked through the door. And *swoosh*—the butterflies took off in full flight again. What am I going to say? I'm so nervous. I'll mess up my words, and she won't pick us for sure!

A birth mother often wants to meet several couples so she can be sure she has made the best choice possible. That way she can have an inner peace about giving up her baby for adoption. This is a very hard thing for the birth mother to do, and I suggest that you read more about it in the chapter on the birth mother's viewpoint. It will help you understand what she is going through.

Ray and I knew that we were probably being compared with other prospective parents who wanted her baby, and that did not help us feel any better. Sitting in the house talking was awkward, so Ray suddenly said, "Hey, let's go get a milkshake!" We laughed, the tension broke, and we went out the door together. Soon we were all at ease laughing and talking freely about all sorts of things. We were really having a good time. Before leaving, we prayed with this young mother-to-be and drove off.

What an experience! What do you say to the girl who might bear the child who will bring you the fulfillment and happiness you have so longed for? Ray and I didn't even speak until we were about half way home, then we stopped the car to hold hands and pray, "God, have Your way."

A few days later the lawyer called. The girl had really liked us and wanted us to have her baby. This was what we had prayed for. The only problem was that when Ray and I prayed about it together, we didn't have a peace in our hearts. We dearly loved this girl and felt like we were best friends— but the peace would not come.

There was another factor. The lawyer wanted $6,000 up front. We had prayed and said, "God, if You want us to have this baby, then You will provide the money." But the money had not come. As heartbreaking as it was, we felt this was not our baby. It was very hard for us to call the lawyer and tell him our decision, especially since our greatest desire was to have a child. But we could not deny the lack of peace we felt God had placed in our hearts.

A Matter of Money

The weeks that followed were troubling. The butterflies became vicious hornets from Satan. "You made the wrong decision . . . Now you'll never have a baby," and on and on.

During this period I was working part time, devoting the rest of my time to being a pastor's wife and ministering together with Ray. We have been a team, pastoring as partners since we were first married. Now we had a large singles' ministry of nearly eight hundred singles, and it was very time consuming.

Again and again the amount of $6,000 kept ringing in my mind. I wanted to have the money ready when God did bring the right child into our lives. I knew God would have to provide, yet I felt I had to do what I could. So I began working full time in addition to ministering with my husband. I became very frugal, saving every penny, not buying anything but the bare necessities.

Our church was in the midst of a new building project, and we were very excited about it. Ray and I faithfully gave our tithe in addition to special offerings for different needs, especially those for missionaries. Our tithes of ten percent went straight to our local church, and the offerings, sometimes five, ten or fifteen percent, were given as God spoke to us.

One night I was trying to unwind and relax after a long hard day of work for both of us. It had climaxed with ministry that evening to our singles' group. Ray came to me and said, "Becky, I've got something to tell you. I feel prompted that we should step out in faith and give $6,000 toward the building project."

What? Had I heard him right? "$6,000?" I screamed. "We give our ten percent faithfully and extra offerings besides. Isn't that enough?" And I blew up!

At that point all Ray said was, "Becky, go to prayer and tell me tomorrow." And he fell sound asleep.

I went out into the living room, crying furiously. "What do You want, God? We couldn't have children, and we gave up that right. Then You gave us hope that You heard our prayers by allowing two people to call. We asked *You* for $6,000 to help provide a child, and You didn't supply it Now You're asking *us* to give You $6,000? I don't understand, and I can't do it, God. I just can't do it! I've been working so hard to raise the money, and You want us to give it up. That means it will be twice as long before we will have money enough to adopt. Oh, God, You can't ask this of us," I cried.

I sobbed and pleaded all night until I could cry no more. Yet what I felt in my heart was a total surprise. I felt God saying, "Becky, this is what I want." My feelings and emotions weren't saying it, but my heart was. So I told Ray he could start giving toward the building project if he wanted to. I surrendered the $6,000, and once again the right to have children. But, in reality, the money was all God's anyway.

Taking the Risk

Weeks went by, and the phone rang again. It was the contact who had first called the day Ray and I returned from our retreat together. The young mother-to-be was still unsure, but after looking at many couples' resumes, she believed she wanted us to be the parents of her child.

The contact said that they did not know what the total cost would be until the birth, but we would have to start paying for the prenatal expenses right away. They also warned us that we should know up front that if she changed her mind, we could not get any of the money back. That was our risk.

What if this is a con? What if they're setting us up? We don't even know the contact or the girl. What if we lose our money? How can we be sure? These questions began to race through my mind. "We must go to prayer!" Ray said.

Ray and I took the day off and went to the lake. There we wrote out all the pros and cons of an agency adoption, an independent adoption, and an international adoption. Next we wrote down all the pros and cons of this particular situation. Then we went to prayer.

After praying together, we found that we both shared a peace about the situation. Somehow we felt that this was the child for us and that we would have to take the risks. We both had an *inner peace* and an *okay* from the Lord. Yes, there were a lot of risks, but life is full of risks. We cannot let our fears hold us back, otherwise we'll never accomplish anything in life.

We called the contact back and sent off a check to cover the prenatal costs. Now it was time to wait since the baby would not be born for six more months. The birth mother wanted us to come and meet her as soon as possible. She lived quite a distance away and we couldn't take any more time off until our vacation, so we set up a meeting for then.

In the meantime, we learned that she wanted us to be in the delivery room with her so she could place the child right into our hands. We were so excited! I had always wanted to have natural childbirth and had keenly felt the disappointment of knowing I never would. Now I was going to have the opportunity to be a part of it. We quickly said yes.

We agreed we would come down on our vacation and meet her. Then when the baby was ready to be born, we would fly back immediately as soon as they called. We would have our bags all packed and ready to go so we could leave at a moment's notice.

Now all we had to do was *wait*!

I'll let Ray finish telling you the rest of our story.

In His Hands

Everything happened so rapidly. A week earlier than expected we found ourselves standing in the lobby of the Southern California Hospital waiting for the rather sudden arrival of the child we would soon adopt.

Our plan had been to meet the mother and become more acquainted prior to finalizing the adoption. However, seven days before the due date the mother went into early labor with some very dangerous complications. The umbilical cord had been wrapped around the baby's neck, and trauma had ensued. Everyone was concerned. It was a troubled delivery, with the possibility of performing a cesarean section.

Earlier that day, Rebecca and I had held hands and agreed that God would supernaturally intervene. We felt God had told us to adopt this particular child, and we knew the baby was in His hands.

There were also other factors to consider. When you go through an independent adoption all the medical costs are paid by the adoptive parents. God had provided miraculously up until now. However, complications quickly accelerate the cost of childbirth, and we could have been put in a dangerous financial position.

Miraculously, the birth was completed, and everybody was fine. The child was kept in the hospital three days under careful supervision because of the traumatic birth. Yet, everything went according to plan, and we knew God was at work. A few days later we took the beautiful baby boy home.

Rebecca had to fly home with the baby immediately because of his condition. I drove alone to our Northern California home. But the hours slipped by quickly as I anticipated the joy and thrill of getting to know my new son.

It was a miracle, especially in a country where there are six hundred parents to one adoptive child and where medical treatment can be exorbitant for even simple procedures. Yet all the costs were within the financial provision God had supplied.

The Lord had led us to use independent adoption this time. We followed, obeyed, prayed, and did what was required of us. Everything went according to the plan He prearranged. Our miracle became a beautiful testimony to our church, friends, and to hundreds of infertile couples hoping for a way out of their seemingly impossible situation.

Two Years Later

After the birth of our adopted son, Rebecca and I had the opportunity to pursue two other independent adoptions. But God gave us no peace in our hearts about either situation, so we did not proceed.

The summer after our little boy turned two, my wife received an impression that by the fall we would have another child in our home. Knowing this could be our last summer alone with our son, we planned a special vacation.

Two days before leaving, we received a call from Bethany Christian Services, with whom we had made contact several years before. Although we had kept all doors open, we were not considering an agency adoption at this time. Our first adoption had gone well, and we assumed we would take the independent route again.

The social worker at Bethany said they had received a phone call about a little girl who was up for adoption. Rebecca and I immediately began to reconsider. When we told the social worker our vacation plans, she said we were headed to the very city where the child was in a foster home.

After a wonderful week of playing and having fun with our son, we ended our vacation by picking up the new addition to our family—a beautiful baby girl.

Once again, God supplied all the money and arranged all the details. The adoption went smoothly as the Lord had promised. For days, Rebecca and I walked around in awe of God's goodness and faithfulness, amazed to be the parents of a lovely daughter in such a short time.

Our story clearly indicates that God is the Giver of children. His promises are true, and His gifts are perfect. You, too, can trust our loving heavenly Father for your own miracle.

CHAPTER THIRTEEN

Independent Adoptions

After Ray and I had successfully searched for a child independently, people began to seek us out for information on what to do. I shared what I had learned and made copies of all the material I had accumulated.

Phone calls, letters, and pleas for help began to come to me from childless couples who had nowhere else to turn. Then I began to realize the importance of putting all this information, along with our experiences, into a book. I prayed and asked the Lord to confirm this leading of my heart.

Not long after I had prayed for direction, I was standing looking through the shelves of a Christian bookstore. A young couple came in and with tears pleaded with the salesperson for some kind of book or information on how to find a baby to adopt. The salesclerk had to tell them that the store did not have any Christian books addressing their problem and how to solve it. That incident was my answer from the Lord.

I began to collect additional information and gather incidents and stories that would provide guidelines for procedures and also offer helpful suggestions from those with firsthand experience.

Why Go it Alone?

After running into closed doors and dead ends with agencies, many couples turn to independent adoption. Other couples, who are reluctant to battle the bureaucratic system, decide to by-pass the agencies altogether and start with independent adoption.

The primary advantage to independent adoption is that parents can find a child in far less time than they will through most agencies. Another factor is that there are generally fewer restrictions for prospective parents.

While agencies deal with children of all ages, more babies are available through independent adoption. There are several reasons for this.

Birth mothers are turning more and more to independent channels because they have someone to provide financial support during the pregnancy and pay for hospital fees. In addition, they can participate in the choice of the baby's adoptive parents after meeting and getting to know them. Most birth mothers want to approve prospective parents before they are willing to give their babies up for adoption.

Private or independent adoptions now account for approximately half of all adoptions in California. This method of obtaining a child is legal in all states except Connecticut, Delaware, Minnesota, Michigan, and Massachusetts. But the laws are changing rapidly, so it's best to check with your local social services office about the regulations in your state.

Making Contacts

If you choose to pursue the independent route, you will have to locate someone who can provide a child for adoption. There are several ways to accomplish this.

Many small, private agencies have sprung up across the country that use a combination of both agency and independent methods. Some place an ad in the classified section of the newspaper seeking unwed mothers who want to give up their babies. Others are an outgrowth of local homes for unwed mothers or crisis pregnancy centers. They probably will not advertise this fact, but your pastor or local pro-life organization may be able to give you information about them.

Another way to locate a birth mother is through personal contact. Infertility is a private problem, but you must overcome your inhibitions and be willing to talk to anyone who might be able to help you find a child—physicians, social workers, pastors, other adoptive parents, etc.

Contact them by phone, letter, or in person and tell them of your situation and your desire to adopt. Have something to give them—a resume, a letter, or a picture of yourselves with a brief history on the back. In addition, ask them for further leads. While one doctor may not be able to help you, he may know of another physician who can. Build a network of people who know about your situation.

One couple, who was unable to adopt through an agency due to the husband's age, launched a massive personal letter writing campaign to over seven hundred obstetricians and churches. In each letter they included a color snapshot of themselves and personal information. They were candid about the husband's age, their Christian lifestyle, and their desire to find a child to love. While some couples have had very little response from this type of appeal, this couple found themselves the parents of a darling baby boy within three months.

Locating an adoptable baby is like searching for employment. Often the most impressive resume wins the interview. During our search, I compiled materials and developed a resume to use in making contact with a pregnant woman considering adoption for her baby. I have also helped other couples make up resumes that resulted in successful adoptions.

This is the letter that Ray and I sent to physicians, pastors, crisis pregnancy centers, etc.

To Whom It May Concern:

My wife and I are interested in adopting children. Even before we discovered our infertility, we always wanted to offer a loving home to children.

In January of 1982, I went through part of our extensive medical testing. The tests showed an absence of the vas deferens tube, thus eliminating any chance of biological children. However, we still have a sincere desire to raise a family and therefore wish to adopt another child. We adopted our first child in January, 1983.

Please place our resume in your file and should you know of a child, feel free to call us any time of the day or night. We can be contacted at home (phone number) or at my office (phone number).

Thank you for your time and consideration.

Cordially,

Mr. and Mrs. Ray Larson

Our ideas on how to write a cover letter and formulate a resume are found in Appendix III.

If locating a child is as important to you as finding a good job, then you'll realize that the resume approach is well worth the time and effort involved in writing, printing, and mailing. You may be surprised at the number of contacts you receive from this method.

Another method of locating a birth mother starts with placing a personal ad in the classified section of the newspaper. While we do not recommend this method neither do we condemn it. Surely the lives of many babies have been saved because women in a crisis pregnancy situation saw an ad and decided not to have an abortion.

You can find examples of ads in your local or city newspaper like the following:

> Happily married Christian couple unable to have baby wishes to adopt newborn. We can give a child a beautiful home, lots of love, and a chance to have the best things in life. Strictly legal and confidential. Will pay all medical and living expenses if appropriate. Please give yourself, your baby and us a happier future. Call collect.

Another ad began similar to the one above and then finished with: "We will pay all your expenses for a new start and make this difficult time easier for you. Write to Box 100."

While these ads can provide birth mothers with a link to you, they are also excellent sources of leads for black market baby brokers. If you choose this way of reaching a birth mother, be sure to work with a reputable attorney. Use caution, wisdom, and utmost discretion.

Paid advertising for a prospective baby to adopt is illegal in some states, so be aware of the laws before you place your ad.

The Legal Aspects

Once you have begun to initiate leads, a birth parent may contact you. At this point you need a lawyer, a doctor, or a pastor to act as an intermediary between yourself and the birth mother. Although she is the one who will choose the family for her child, you need someone who can represent your interests in an objective manner.

When I began to seek information about private adoption, I found that a lot of attorneys would not even talk to me without a nonrefundable prepayment ranging anywhere from $75 to $200. The first lawyer Ray and I went to see wanted us to pay $6,000 up front with no guarantee of a baby or a refund.

It is sad that the infertile couple who is already hurting must put up with this kind of mercenary approach to receiving any help. Ask the Lord to lead you to a compassionate lawyer who can give you the advice you need. But make sure you don't proceed any further without legal counsel.

When selecting a lawyer, choose one who has had experience in adoptions. Ask other adoptive parents for recommendations and how much you can expect to pay for the attorney's services. Even if you have a good attorney, you should research the laws regarding independent adoption in your state for yourself.

Find out the requirements regarding release forms that must be obtained from the birth mother and father. The birth father as well as the mother may have to sign the form, and if his location is unknown, you may need to advertise for the birth father. It is illegal for anyone other than the natural parent(s) to actually place the child.

Later, the state department of social services' adoption unit will conduct a home study, obtain information to determine if the child is legally free for adoption, and provide some post-placement services. They also guarantee that the conditions of the adoption are understood by everyone involved.

The law stipulates that no one is allowed to make a profit on a private or independent adoption. The medical costs, expenses resulting directly from the pregnancy (prenatal care, anything related to the baby, etc.), and legal or professional fees are the only expenses allowed. You should keep all receipts for any expenditures related to the birth and adoption. During the home study, you will have to prove you paid them. They are also tax deductible in some states.

As you begin talking with a lawyer and birth mother, be sure everyone concerned agrees on what you will be paying for and what you won't be paying for. It is at this point that confusion and misunderstanding can result and cause complications later.

Make sure it is the birth mother's choice to give up her child, or she could go to court some day and say she was forced into the adoption. Be absolutely certain that she is willing to sign the consent form to place the baby in the adoptive parents' home with an intent to sign a relinquishment.

At this point the adoptive parents are in a risky situation because the birth mother can reclaim the child any time prior to signing the relinquishment. The relinquishment, once signed, however, may be revoked in most states only upon court findings that the withdrawal will be best for the child or that there has been misrepresentation on the part of the adoptive parents.

The signing of the relinquishment usually takes place two to six months after placement. This varies from state to state. For example, one state requires a guardianship period of more than a year after placement during which time the birth mother can reclaim her child.

If the birth mother decides to reclaim her child, she is not responsible to pay back any of the expenses of her pregnancy, delivery, or legal fees. The prospective parents have no way to recoup the money they have spent. At this point adopting through an agency has an advantage over independent channels. Once an agency places a child with a family, the birth mother cannot reclaim the child.

One girl, soon due to give birth, received a copy of our resume. She liked us and felt she wanted us to have her baby, but making the final decision was very hard for her.

Ray and I felt we should get an attorney and stay removed from another emotionally draining situation. We had our lawyer make all the contacts. He said things looked good and he would contact us when the baby was ready to take home.

We were anxiously awaiting his call when we decided to check with the hospital ourselves. They told us the baby had already been born. Immediately, a social worker got on the phone and, to our great shock, told us the girl had changed her mind.

Ray and I cried together at first, but then realized that it was a decision the girl had to make for herself because she would live with it. We had paid $500 in advance expenses—which we lost—but we acknowledged to one another that this was a risk we had been willing to take.

The Final Hurdle

As you wait for the birth, you should be preparing to bring the baby into your home. You will need to designate a nursery area, purchase baby clothes, and choose a boy's name and a girl's name.

In most cases you will take the child home with you the same day the mother is released from the hospital. You will need proper identification since you will be asked to sign a hospital release form, which is a receipt for custody of the child. Ask for a copy of the form because this becomes temporary proof of your right and authorization to treat the child medically.

Your attorney will prepare a petition for adoption. A signed copy should be sent to your state department of social services' adoption unit who will then contact you for an interview. If you have not been contacted or interviewed by this agency within sixty days of the baby's birth, you should advise your lawyer.

After you have been interviewed, social services will interview the natural mother, obtain her consent to adopt, and conduct one or more home visits. Following this, the agency will usually prepare and file its final report with the court recommending the adoption. The adoption is usually finalized in six to ten months.

This is generally the most emotionally trying time of the adoption since the mother may change her mind prior to its finalization. This is why counseling for the birth mother prior to her decision to give consent to adopt is so important. She should understand the responsibility and the consequence of her decision prior to this emotional point in the adoption procedure.

I read a story about a couple who tried for nine years to adopt. After working through all of the agency red tape with no success, they tried the independent route. They finally located a young girl and made all the arrangements. In the end, after this couple had paid all the medical and legal bills, the young mother decided to keep the baby.

But this couple didn't quit. Later, another contact led to a successful adoption, and they were given a baby boy. This couple related how happy they were to pick up their son at the hospital and how much he has meant to their lives. They said the money, the rejections, the red tape, and the long wait were well worth the joy and blessing they had received in return.

What do they say to couples who are discouraged and disillusioned? "Hang in there and don't give up."

Minimizing the Risks

Our darling little boy brought great joy to our hearts, but we didn't want him to grow up as an only child. I especially wanted to have a little girl, too. This feeling was intensified by having several lovely nieces whom I love like my own. One day when I was praying about this longing for a baby girl, I felt the Lord was saying He had heard my prayers and someday He would give me the desires of my heart—but in *His* time.

About a week later, a phone call came describing a woman who had just had a baby girl—now three weeks old. She had decided to give the baby up for adoption and wanted to meet us. Our contact asked if we could come right away.

Ray and I had a good friend fly us in his private plane to meet the young mother the following morning. The baby girl was beautiful. As we talked with the birth mother and her family, all the initial tension melted away, making us feel we'd known each other for years. We stayed a few hours, discussing names, arrangements, ourselves, and much more.

As we prepared to leave, I took this young mother's hand and said, "Do what you feel you must; it will be okay. I know it is a hard decision, and I'll be praying for you." Then we all prayed together for God's will to be done and left.

Ray and I talked excitedly all the way home about how everything seemed so perfect. We talked about the baby, what we would need to do, and an upcoming shower that our friend's daughter had already planned.

Everything was set, but somehow that inner peace was missing from my heart. I knew God had said that He had heard my prayer for a little girl, but was this the child? I prayed and prayed the next day, but the peace was still missing. Finally, when we couldn't wait any longer, we called and were told the mother had denied us.

Denied us! Oh, how those words hurt at first. But when I thought about it, I realized that the peace and assurance had been missing from my own heart. This child was not God's will for us. So we praised God and moved on.

Because there weren't any financial ties with the mother, it was easier for us to accept her decision. But being turned down is never easy. This time we had told very few people that we were looking into a specific adoption opportunity. That made it much easier on us emotionally. At least we didn't have to explain the rejection to everyone.

It is important to pray about any possibility to adopt that is presented to you. Go ahead and meet every prospective birth mother, taking advantage of any opportunity. As you pray and seek God's peace in your heart, try not to get your hopes too high. Ask God to close the door if it is not His will.

We also recommend that you don't tell too many people about specific opportunities, except perhaps a close friend or relative who will pray with you. Explaining to twenty people why the adoption fell through can be an agonizing experience. Don't put yourself in that situation.

Try to keep a positive attitude even if one or more opportunities ends unsuccessfully. God hears your prayers and will answer them in His timing. Don't let the experience cause you to become bitter and discouraged. Learn to trust God and praise Him whatever the outcome. He knows what is best for you, the child, and the birth mother.

Here are some guidelines on how to minimize the risks.

1. Research all the laws on independent adoption in your state, including laws governing the rights of the birth father as well as the birth mother. In some states, the birth grandparents also have rights.

2. Write letters to everyone—adoptive parent groups, doctors, pastors, and family court judges.

3. Select a lawyer experienced with independent adoptions. Check his references, find out how many adoptions he has successfully completed for clients. Be sure that your state's laws allow for any adoption fees that he might charge. If you are adopting a child from another state, make sure your lawyer can handle the legalities of interstate adoption.

4. Insist that your attorney obtain complete medical histories of the birth parents and both sets of grandparents before signing any agreement.

5. If you meet directly with the birth mother, meet in a neutral place such as a restaurant, your lawyer's office, or a pastor's office.

6. Do not pay any money beyond the attorney's fees and the mother's direct pregnancy and birth expenses. After the child is in your home, you may feel obligated or out of gratitude want to help the birth mother financially. If you give money to her beyond the actual medical expenses, you can be held liable for extortion. In some states, the child could be removed from your home. Don't get trapped in this innocent but dangerous predicament.

7. Ask a pediatrician to examine the baby and make sure all necessary tests have been conducted before you take custody.

Although the risks are obvious, your security in any venture lies with the Lord and not with the circumstances. If you are trusting God, seeking His will at every turn, asking Him for that inner peace, and obtaining the proper counsel, the adoptive experience will develop into an adventure in faith and a stepping-stone to spiritual growth.

CHAPTER FOURTEEN

Mothers at Heart

Ray and I were sitting in a group of about fifty people when the subject of adoption came up. A woman said, "I don't understand how a mother can give her child away. She must not care about her baby or she would have kept him."

This statement sparked something deep inside me, and I felt I had to respond. "I don't mean to be blunt," I said, "but your statement is absolutely wrong. Birth mothers love their children enough to give them life. Most of them place their babies up for adoption because they want their child to have a better life than they, as a single parent, can give them. If they didn't care, they could have easily aborted them."

Many unwed, pregnant women find themselves in an emotional pressure cooker. They may be unable to stand up to the stress of a disapproving family or the thought of raising and supporting a child all alone. At this very difficult time, they find themselves faced with options that are all very serious, complicated, and permanent. No wonder so many of them make the wrong choice.

One girl said, "I had an abortion because it made everything complete. If I had given the baby up for adoption, I would have lived these past years in agony wondering if my child was all right."

A Heartrending Decision

For some young women, the prospect of adoption can be as heartbreaking as abortion. Most birth mothers agonize over their decision to give their baby up for adoption.

A sixteen-year-old birth mother who spent her pregnancy in a maternity home intended to give the baby up for adoption. She entered the delivery room full of fear, clutching her gingham doll. Four days later she sat in the hospital chapel trying to prepare herself to sign the adoption papers. She was asked if she had read the papers, if she understood them, and if she realized she could never change her mind once she signed them. She was also asked if anyone, at the home or otherwise, had put pressure on her to give up her baby.

The young girl signed the papers and then saw her baby for the first and last time just before the adoptive parents arrived to receive him. As she tenderly cuddled the baby in her arms, he opened his eyes and stared deep into hers. Then she began to cry and called for the nurse to take him because she couldn't stand holding him any longer. Her only stipulation to the adoptive parents was that the baby be told she did love him but, because she wanted the best for him, she allowed him to be adopted.

One birth mother almost reversed her decision to allow her baby to be adopted. Here's how she described her feelings:

> As the court date got closer and closer, I became more and more frightened. Finally, I called my social worker and told her I wanted to see the baby one more time before I actually signed the final papers. She asked me if I realized what this would do to the adoptive parents who had had him for

two months—how traumatic it would be for them. I said I didn't care; I had to see him once more.

The meeting was set up in my social worker's office. But as soon as I held him in my arms, I realized that he wasn't mine anymore. He was being loved by different people in a different way, but I knew it was right. I just needed to touch him and say goodbye. Even now, more than a year later, I feel like I'm on an emotional roller coaster sometimes, but I remind myself that I couldn't give him the security that he has now. I couldn't deny my child that right.

Our social worker says that it is the younger teenagers, the girls between thirteen and seventeen, who change their minds and keep the child. These girls are often confused and fail to recognize problems that can arise in the future. A lot of them just want to be loved themselves. More mature pregnant women, however, usually go through with the adoption procedure. They are more inclined to base their decision on the child and his/her welfare.

Agencies and groups working with birth mothers who have been allowed to participate in the selection of the adoptive parents have made a surprising conclusion. When some form of ongoing contact is established, it is rare that the birth mother changes her mind and demands her baby back. Just having some sort of contact with the family seems to relieve the birth mother's mind tremendously.

Most birth mothers have a deep love and concern for their child that never ends. They only want to know that the child is loved and well cared for.

One birth mother, after reconciling herself to her decision, said, "Meeting and telling the adoptive parents that they were going to be my baby's mom and dad, after they had waited so long for a child, was the neatest thing I have ever done."

One adoptive couple said, "We went through great pain and frustration wanting children yet knowing we couldn't have any of our own. When I met the birth mother, we realized she had been through an incredible amount of pain herself in coming to the choice of releasing her baby for adoption. We felt that we were there for her and she was there for us; we all had deep needs and could fulfill them for each other in this beautiful way."

Open Adoption

In an open adoption, the birth mother relinquishes all legal, moral, and nurturing rights to the child, but she retains some degree of right to continuing contact and an ongoing knowledge of the child's upbringing. Many birth mothers want to break the myth that they don't care about the child they are giving up for adoption.

Open adoption involves varying degrees of contact between the birth mother (and sometimes the birth father), the adoptive parents, and the child. Contact may take place when the adoptive parents pick up the child at the hospital and go no further. Or it may involve an openness where there is ongoing communication but no personal contact. Some couples and birth mothers have worked out arrangements that involve continued communication and access to one another throughout the years the adopted child lives with the adoptive parents.

All private adoptions are open adoptions to some degree, but many agencies try to avoid any contact between the birth parent and the adoptive parents. Some authorities argue that if the confidentiality of closed records is not maintained, the birth mother loses the security of knowing she can get on with her life without worrying that her decision might later come back to haunt her. They feel if she does not have such an assurance, the birth mother may decide to abort the baby.

The other side argues that an open adoption relieves the birth mother of the pain of giving up her baby to complete strangers with no further knowledge of the child's welfare. They feel this helps young women choose adoption over abortion.

One adoptee, who was also a birth mother who gave her child up for adoption, felt that many women refuse to surrender their babies to be adopted because they cannot cope with never seeing the child again.

Some older children are caught in limbo in foster homes because their birth parents will not terminate their parental rights for fear they will never see their children again. Open adoption might make it possible for these children to find a real and permanent family of their own.

An agency that uses open adoption feels that the birth mother works through her stages of grief more quickly and easily after meeting the adoptive parents. She comes to a peace about her decision sooner than women who have no idea what the adoptive parents are like.

It has been suggested that more birth mothers might consider adoption if they were allowed to feel they were a part not only of the process of adoption but also of the ongoing progress of the child. This could also decrease the adopted child's sense of rejection by his birth mother. As part of this new approach to adoption, some groups are urging that all adoption records be fully open to the child when they become an adult.

On the other hand, some experts think that ongoing contact with birth parents can be too confusing for the child and damage the security he or she needs in having only one set of parents. As a compromise, some parties have been willing to agree to a form of independent adoption with no contact between the birth mother and the child and adoptive parents, but with all records kept open for everyone involved.

Dealing With Your Fears

The idea of open adoption can create fear in some adoptive parents. It's often difficult and sometimes threatening to deal with having another person involved in your child's life. But other couples view open adoption as a planning and information exchange between two sets of caring parents.

Bethany Christian Services had us respond to each statement on the following Adoption Questionnaire on Openness:

1. I would like to meet the birth mother/father, one time, with no identifying information shared, *before* birth so that she/we can feel comfortable about us/her. Response:

2. I would like to meet the birth mother/father, one time, with no identifying information shared, *only after* papers are signed and she has no legal recourse to change her mind. Response:

3. I would like the birth mother to talk with us over the phone (a Bethany Christian Services' worker would dial the number) *before birth.* Response:

4. I don't mind if the birth mother is shown/given a picture of us before or after deciding on us as parents. Response:

5. We/I would be willing to answer a letter written by the birth mother *before* birth and placement. Response:

6. I would send one, two or three pictures of our child to the agency up to age __ to be shared with the birth mother. Response:

These are difficult issues for adoptive parents to deal with. Some couples will not even consider the risks involved at all. Yet, open adoption does not change the fact that once relinquishments are signed and a child is placed with you, the birth parent cannot reclaim the child.

I like the idea of meeting the birth mother and/or father even though it is emotionally trying. I also believe, however, that there comes a time to cut off all contact.

Personally, Ray and I believe that contact should last no later than the end of the first year. We feel it is too confusing to the child to have both the birth mother and the real mother in the child's life.

In the first few chapters of her book, *And With the Gift Came Laughter*, Ann Kiemel Anderson shares about her special relationship with the two birth mothers who wanted Ann and Will to adopt their babies. Yet, the limits for contact were set from the beginning, and the birth mothers knew the time would come when they had to say goodbye. This unique and heartwarming story unveils the risks involved and the joys that result from complete surrender.

With God's help, you can find the best method of open adoption for all concerned in your unique situation. Don't try to pattern someone else's experience. God knows what you can handle, and only He knows what the future holds. Let Him help you make this difficult decision. Don't agree to something that you can't live with or may regret years later.

Picking Parents

Most agencies now allow the birth mother to see several potential adopting family histories in order to choose the parents for her child. The following information is typical of the profile information you will be asked to provide for the birth mother to view.

1. How/why did you come to pursue adoption? What are your thoughts about birth parents? Share any experience you may have had with adoption. Also share what this child will mean to your family—blessings, etc. Basically, birth parents are looking for reassurance that this child will be loved and cared for as they would if they were able. This assurance means a great deal coming from the parents who will be taking on this responsibility.

2. Spiritual commitment: Your denominational affiliation and any activities/involvement within or outside your church. Summarize/highlight primary spiritual guidelines you will use in rearing and teaching your child.

3. Express your basic philosophy about parenting.

4. Your ages.

5. Number of years married and brief description of husband/wife relationship.

6. Any children? Their role and place in the family.

7. Physical description: Coloring, height, weight, and frame size.

8. Employment: Field or type of work. Current and also relevant past experience that has shaped your goals, awareness, or thinking.

9. Educational experience: Number of years, subjects enjoyed and majored in. Other activities and involvement in school.

10. Hobbies and leisure activities: What do you do for fun or to relax? If you like, you might even describe a typical day or weekend for your family. What are some things you plan/dream for the future?

Adamant about wanting the best thing for her baby, one young, unwed mother was very realistic about her future in trying to raise the child herself. She knew that the family she had chosen deeply desired a child and that they were ready to parent. It gave her great assurance to know they had much more to offer the child than she did. When she was ready to give birth, she asked the adoptive parents to be present in the delivery room. In a true gesture of love, she gently handed over the newly born baby to the adoptive mother.

One adoptive couple recalled that when they met the birth mother for the first time, they all hugged each other and began to cry. The adoptive mother tried to get the birth mother to stop crying, fearing she would cause herself distress and pain. When the birth mother responded, "It's okay, I'm crying because I'm happy you will be the ones to get my baby," this childless couple was thrilled and relieved beyond words.

My husband and I highly esteem any birth mother who chooses to give her baby to a loving family instead of aborting the child or trying to raise the child by herself when she cannot. Because of the bond that develops between mother and baby during pregnancy and birth, the decision to give the child a better life requires a selfless and loving heart. The myth that those who release their babies just don't care about them is just that—an ugly myth.

One young girl living in a Christian group home for unwed mothers said,

> Once I got over my initial shock and fear, I felt a great sense of responsibility for the little life inside of me. I really wanted to be this child's mother, but I also wanted what was best for him. When I prayed to the Lord, the answer was painful, but clear to me. I placed my child in the Lord's hands to give to a couple who could love and care for him better than I could. This did not mean I lacked the desire to be a mother. It was painful to see him in the hospital nursery for the last time because I loved him so, but it was small pain compared to the joy of knowing he had a complete life ahead of him.

Mother to Mother

A birth mother will always wonder, "How is my baby doing? Do the adoptive parents love him/her as much as I do? Is he/she healthy and happy?" A letter can answer some of her questions and help the young woman move on with her life. It helps her feel she made the right choice.

I believe it is important for the adoptive parents to write and let the birth mother know how much she is appreciated and that everything is well with the baby. Sometimes a picture can be sent with the letter. Below is a letter sent to a birth mother.

> To a very special person:
>
> Where do I begin? If you could see my heart, I think you would understand me more. First of all, we (I'm also speaking for my husband) want

to say thank you for giving us a gift of love. Your son (we named him Joshua) is a gift from God. As you can see from the picture, he is an adorable baby with his curly, blond hair and baby-blue eyes. He weighs fourteen pounds and is about twenty-three inches long.

On March 1st, we dedicated him at our church, and he slept through the whole service. He is a very good baby but has his temper, especially when he is hungry. Except for a cold he had a few weeks ago, he is very healthy.

The reason for this letter is to tell you how much we appreciate you. We respect the decision you made and know it was very hard for you. You will always have a special place in our hearts for what you have done in giving Joshua life and giving us such a wonderful blessing. When Joshua is mature enough, we will give him the letter you wrote to him. We want him to know how much you cared for him and why you chose adoption.

We promise you we will always love and cherish Joshua for the rest of our lives. He is a dream come true to us. We will continue to pray for you and ask God's blessing on your life.

We wish you happiness in the future.

Sincerely,
The Adoptive Mother

This type of letter helps the birth mother cope with having made the decision to surrender her child for adoption. It also helps her to be sure that her decision was right when she selected the adoptive parents. She can see that they are real people, with real feelings, not just some "make believe" couple the agency or contact made up. Letters can bridge the gap between the birth mother and the adoptive parents and help bring peace to their hearts.

When an unmarried mother decides to give her child up for adoption, it is the ultimate gift of love. One adoptive mother was quoted as saying, "I have no way of even imagining what it would be like to give up a baby. I only know she did it out of love for her child, and I love her for that."

The prayer of one adoptive mother sums up the gratitude of those who have received the gift of life through adoption: "Dear God, please bless the girl who gave birth to my child. Give her strength and happiness. In some way, let her know our mutual son is happy, safe, and loved. Wherever she is, let her know she is loved, too."

A successful adoption will be a blessing to everyone concerned. When the birth mother can release her baby to parents whom she knows will love and care for her child, she feels confident and pleased by her decision. The couple is blessed by God's wonderful gift of a child, and their hearts are filled with gratitude toward the birth mother for allowing them to have this precious life. And the child receives the care and affection of loving parents as he grows up in a secure home and family.

Let me end this chapter with a glimpse into the heart of a young girl in trouble. Here, in her own words, she describes her experience:

> When I first suspected I was pregnant, I thought I would just die. It was absolutely the worst thing that could happen to me, and I knew my parents wouldn't be able to handle it.
>
> I had just turned sixteen and had been sexually active for awhile. But I wasn't a hard type of person—I just wanted to be accepted. I hadn't had any long-term relationships, and it never

dawned on me that I might get pregnant.

Six weeks into the pregnancy I went to the hospital because of some internal bleeding related to the pregnancy. I tried to keep everything a secret from my folks. I planned to have an abortion at the same time that the doctors were operating on my insides, but through a strange turn of events, which I see now as the hand of God, I came out of the operating room still pregnant.

A kind nurse at the hospital convinced me to call my parents and tell them what was going on. My mom and dad were shocked and hurt. It was the only time I ever saw my dad cry. The next month and a half that I lived at home was very hard on all of us.

My mother arranged for me to go to a home for unwed mothers. It was the first time I'd been away from my mom and dad for any length of time, and I was very homesick. Nearly all the other girls at the home came from broken and hurtful backgrounds. Many were insecure and didn't care to reach out to me and be friendly. I had to earn respect there.

Most of the girls came to the home around their seventh or eighth month of pregnancy, but I arrived in my third. Although those six months were probably the hardest of my life—being away from my family, friends, and familiar surroundings—it was an invaluable experience. I learned to appreciate a lot of things I had taken for granted before, and I tried to make the most out of a difficult situation.

The home where I was living set me up with a case worker from an adoption agency. She was very nice, and we met once a week. She repeatedly warned me about private adoptions and the evils thereof. Meanwhile, my mother was contacting churches, trying to find someone to visit me and encourage me.

One day a nice Christian doctor called me and asked if I'd like to have my baby put in a Christian home. "Aha!" I thought. "I've been warned about you," and very coldly cut our conversation short. But for the next few weeks I could not get his idea out of my mind. I finally ended up calling him and agreed to adopt through him. The decision gave me great peace and joy. But when I happily told my case worker, she went into a tirade about what a horrible thing I had done and my lack of responsibility in the whole matter. I left in tears not believing that this was the same person who had become a friend.

As my due date approached, I didn't give it much thought because most of the girls were weeks later than the date the doctors had determined. Going into labor sort of caught me off guard, and I was surprised when I delivered an 8 lb. 8 oz. girl on January 10—the same date the doctors had given me.

I remember holding my baby and thinking that I had really done the right thing in not aborting her, but being equally sure that I was doing the right thing in putting her up for adoption. In my own way, I felt I was providing her with a mother and a father.

January tenth never slips by me unnoticed, and it is a good feeling to know there is a little girl out there getting a chance at life. That's something I will never regret.

CHAPTER FIFTEEN

Special Kinds of Adoption

Thousands of unloved, desperate children around the world are praying, "Dear God, please send someone to adopt me." Could you be the answer to a child's prayer?

God can take your need to have children and make it the solution for a lonely, hurting child—one who longs to have parents he or she can call, "Mommy and Daddy." Open your heart as we share two ways of adopting children that you may not have considered.

Adopting a Foreign Child

Foreign adoption appeals to those who do not fall within the general agency restrictions or who do not want to wait up to seven years for a baby. Although the process involves a monumental amount of red tape, these children can be adopted sometimes within six months and usually after no longer than two years. The older the child, the shorter the waiting period.

Because there are not enough adoptable children available in the United States, the number of foreign adoptions rises each year. Americans adopted more than 8,000 children from foreign countries in 1983, up from approximately 5,000 foreign adoptions the previous year.

There are two ways to adopt internationally: through an agency or privately. If you wish to adopt privately, there are several groups that specialize in helping couples deal with the foreign complexities of an international adoption. These groups are not adoption agencies but are like international contacts for finding children and assisting with an adoption. We have provided the names and addresses of these groups in Appendix IV.

Before proceeding, be sure to contact your own state department of social services for specific information. Some states do not allow private international adoptions.

Because of the additional risks that can arise in a private international adoption, it is wise to work with an attorney experienced in this area. The language barrier and the complexities of your state working with the international regulations make this kind of adoption a special challenge.

Exchanging information can often be difficult, making communication with your contact person in the foreign country less than satisfying. As a result you may know little about the health of the child, his or her background, or other personal information.

If you feel the Lord is leading you to adopt a foreign child through private channels, you will need to continually put your faith and trust in God to bring you the child He wants you to have. More importantly, you must surrender all your preconceived ideas about the kind of child you desire and be willing to lovingly accept the one chosen for you.

Working With an Agency

In addition to the private groups, many agencies specialize in foreign adoptions. One of the best and most experienced Christian agencies specializing in this field is Holt International. Your local adoption agency should be able to give the names of agencies in your area that handle foreign adoptions.

These agencies generally work through the Intercountry Adoption Program to assist people who want to adopt foreign orphans and babies. Working with one of these agencies is similar to working with a regular adoption agency, except that the procedure is more complex.

The law mandates that anyone wishing to adopt a foreign child must have a home study by a state-designated agency worker. To begin the process, contact an agency specializing in these adoptions and complete a home study.

If you qualify, you will then be shown records and sometimes pictures of available children. Once you choose a child, you will then need to contact the Immigration and Naturalization Service to obtain the forms that will enable your adopted child to legally enter the United States.

If you are dealing with an agency, they will have determined that the child is legally free for adoption and have knowledge of the proper forms that are valid in both the country of the child's birth and in the United States. If you are working privately, the organizations mentioned previously can guide you in determining the child's legal status and the forms needed.

Once the Immigration and Naturalization Service approves the adoption and issues the child a visa, you can arrange to pick up the child or have the child brought to this country.

Foreign adoption on the average costs around $5,000. The amount can vary as can the red tape, depending on the foreign country. Some countries, especially those in Europe, have legal and religious obstacles that prevent foreign adoptions. Most foreign orphans and children adopted within the United States come from Latin America and Asian countries.

Children with Special Needs

Until recently many children without parents were considered unadoptable or "hard to place," due to age, severe medical problems, mixed racial backgrounds, and physical or mental handicaps. These children are now referred to as having "special needs."

While thousands of Americans are adopting children from other countries, there are tens of thousands of American children with special needs waiting to be adopted. They bounce from foster home to foster home or live in institutions without the security of loving, concerned parents. There is evidence, however, that the number of these adoptions have increased in recent years, bringing a glimmer of hope to those who work with these special children.

According to the Office of Human Development Services in the Department of Health and Human Services, there were about 50,000 special needs children available for adoption in 1984. The largest group included those over ten years of age. Some are sibling groups of brothers and sisters who need to be placed together.

Other special needs children include those who are handicapped, both physically and emotionally, and those with mixed racial backgrounds. In spite of their problems, these children have delightful personalities to share with families who can look beyond the labels and love them for who they are—children who want and need a permanent home.

The legislators in our country have come to the realization that it is cost effective to pay governmental subsidies to parents who will adopt special needs children and move them out of expensive foster home programs and publicly supported institutions. Different forms of state and federal financial assistance are available to help provide monthly living expenses as well as medical coverage. This makes it possible for people of moderate or low income—couples who would make excellent parents but who are unable to afford expensive medical care—to adopt children with physical handicaps.

Several agencies and groups assist couples in this kind of adoption by acting as a clearing house for information on available special needs children. We have listed these organizations in Appendix IV.

Special needs children are most often placed through adoption agencies since their needs require a more careful pre-adoption screening process and post-adoption support system than "normal" children do.

Chosen Couples

I believe that God has some very special couples He has prepared to be adoptive parents for these children. If you think you might be one of these couples, then your chances of adopting a child to love are very good.

Prospective parents should be stable in their marriage relationship and have a high degree of flexibility and patience in their personal character. It is helpful if they have strong emotional support from family and friends, a committed social worker, and the companionship of other adoptive parents.

One of the keys to successfully raising a special needs child is to be able to view people for what they *can* accomplish, not what they *cannot*. A child should be seen in relationship to their own individual potential not in comparison with other children. When you stop to think about it, isn't that how our heavenly Father views each of us? What an opportunity for Christian couples to be able to extend the grace, mercy, and love of God to these children.

Prospective parents are carefully screened by agencies to weed out couples who might only be settling for a special needs child because they couldn't get a "perfect" one. No child should ever be a second choice child. Before proceeding with this kind of adoption, be sure you truly want to adopt a young boy or girl who may have problems.

Talk with other adoptive parents to get in touch with your true motivations for this kind of adoption. The North American Council on Adoptable Children (NACAC) provides a link between adoptive parents' groups throughout the United States. (See Appendix IV for their address.)

Nineteen Steps Up the Mountain: The Story of the Debolt Family is one of the best books on this subject. The Debolts have adopted a whole house full of handicapped children. Their story of love and compassion will bring tears to your eyes and open your heart to let God use you in the lives of these special children.

Babies For Sale

The different kinds of adoptions we have discussed in this book are all legitimate and legal—as long as you go through the proper channels and meet all of your state's requirements. There is one kind of "special" adoption, however, that is neither legal nor legitimate.

If you have placed an ad in the newspaper publicizing your desire for a baby, or if you have sent out resumes to strangers, you may be contacted by several people offering their help in finding a child for you. Be very careful and proceed with utmost caution. Don't believe everything they tell you, and ask plenty of questions. If they cannot give you satisfactory answers, don't proceed any further.

Black market adoptions abound when there is a scarcity of infants available for adoption. These "baby brokers" see the opportunity to provide the commodity that childless couples are looking for. They particularly seek out people who seem to be financially well off.

As in all illegal practices, highly unscrupulous people can be involved in baby selling. Since most couples are not experienced in illegal business, they have no idea how to protect themselves when dealing with these brokers.

The people behind the baby black market are a small group of private entrepreneurs, dealers, and middlemen who have made a highly profitable business out of placing children with childless couples. Suitable couples are not sought for homeless children. Instead, couples shop for suitable children. The broker's only criteria is that the couple can pay for the "adoption."

The Baby Trap

Whenever you are involved in an adoption process outside of a well-established agency, be sure you have an experienced lawyer involved. It is wise to obtain the names and addresses of the people you are dealing with, and don't proceed until you have met them in person. Make absolutely sure that you are not involved in the baby black market, no matter what you are promised.

No one is allowed to legally sell their child, but sometimes the payment masquerades under the guise of abnormally high medical and legal costs. Some people, desperate for children, are paying $50,000 to $100,000 for a baby on the black market today.

There is no way to know how many babies are placed each year through "baby brokers," but it is estimated that between 5,000 and 10,000 children change hands illegally. It is possible that some children who have been reported as "missing" are being sold on the black market for adoption.

If you were to adopt a child in this way, you would be forced to commit perjury when the time came to finalize the adoption in court. When the court would request an accounting of your expenses, you would not be able to tell them the truth. If you did, it would be apparent that a black market transaction had taken place. You would then face perjury charges and the resulting penalties. In addition, you would suffer the grief of having the adoption denied and the child taken by the state.

Anyone who pursues an adoption through these channels will spend the rest of their lives in fear that the illegal adoption will be discovered and the child will be taken from them. This fear makes a person highly vulnerable to blackmail as well.

Why would anyone pay up to $50,000 to become involved in an illegal process that could result in their loss of the child at some point? They are generally people who don't fit the standard categories that adoption agencies have for parents. They feel they cannot work through the proper channels—agency or independent. In their desperation and confusion, they become entangled with people who prey upon their broken hearts and take advantage of their plight.

Couples who fall into this trap usually have no knowledge of God's ways. They do not understand how to work with God in His will and timing through the power of faith and prayer. That's why it is so important to seek God's direction at every turn. Don't become so smug, thinking because you know all the ropes that you can leave God out of your decisions. At the same time, don't allow confusion to overtake you and cloud your judgment. Never make any decision when your emotions are consuming you.

Seek the advice of other Christians, and don't try to work in secret. God will honor your openness with wise counsel and protect you from making foolish choices. Remember, His ways are perfect, and with His blessings He brings no trouble nor sorrow. (See Proverbs 10:22.)

CHAPTER SIXTEEN

Searching for Identity

Adoption has become a popular topic. Everywhere you turn today, someone is talking about their experience as an adopted child. Many famous people like Melissa Gilbert, Steven Jobs, Debbie Harry, and pitcher Jim Palmer were adopted as children.

No matter what their background or their present status in life, many adopted people experience the same feelings and ask the same questions: "I wonder who my birth parents are and what they look like." "Why did they choose to give me up for adoption—didn't they love me?" "Do they have the same medical problems I do?"

Adoptive parents must be honest, compassionate, and sympathetic toward a child's need to know about his or her adoption circumstances and birth parents. Dr. James Dobson relates in his book, *The Strong Willed Child,* that telling children they are adopted from the earliest possible moment provides the only solid foundation for their security.

Dr. Dobson recommends that you start telling them about their adoption from the time they begin to beg for stories, perhaps treating their arrival in your home as a wonderful chapter in your family record, using the word adopted in the story until it becomes a synonym for "chosen," "selected," and "wanted."

Always present the adoption as a tremendous blessing that brought great excitement to your house. Tell how you prayed for a child and waited until the news came that the Lord had answered your prayers. You can relate the events surrounding the child's coming into your home—how excited your were, how you called all your friends and relatives about the news, how you prepared a special room and bought toys.

We do not recommend that you *volunteer* other information. Just answer what they are prepared to ask about at the time. Even young children will want to know why their birth mother gave him or her away. You could answer, "Your mother could not take care of you, and she wanted you to have a better life."

I read a second option with a simple change in the wording: "Your mother was not able to take care of *any baby* at that time in her life, so because she loved you, etc." This helps the child to see that it was not something wrong with him or her that caused the relinquishment.

If you keep telling a child that his birth mother gave him up for adoption because she loved him so much, without the further understanding that she could not have possibly taken care of a baby, the child may wonder if *you* might give him up as well because you love him so much.

Who Does the Child Belong To?

As adopted children grow older, it is normal for them to want to search for their biological roots. This may cause the adoptive parents to feel rejected by the child they have chosen to raise as their own. They may begin to doubt their effectiveness as parents, thinking they were not all they should have been or that there must be something they did not do right.

When this happens, many adoptive parents feel their lives are once again slipping out of their hands. They were dependent upon others to assist them through their infertility struggles. During their search for a child, they were at the mercy of people armed with regulations and red tape. Now, after all those years, these parents suddenly feel they have no control over their destiny as they face the possibility of the birth parents coming back into their lives.

Adoptive parents who have never learned the freedom and security that comes from turning their lives over to the rulership of Christ often feel threatened, alarmed, and vulnerable. Christian parents can rest secure, knowing that God is still in control. In their hearts, they know they have done exactly what they set out to do—raise a child in love, nurturing him or her in the ways of the Lord.

No one can take your child from you because that child was not yours to begin with—he or she belongs to the Lord.

Voices From the Past

Being adopted and raised by loving parents can be the best thing that ever happens to a child—and he or she may well be aware of that fact. But the adoptee can still be left with questions and an inner need to "know." This is a normal response, and should not be seen as a threat by the adoptive parents.

Ray and I have agreed that we would help any children we adopt to find their biological parents if this was their desire. We feel strongly, however, that the young person should be twenty-one before any such search is initiated. Prior to that time it is rare that they would have the maturity to cope with an emotional experience of this importance.

At the age of eighteen, youth are just emerging from their teenage years into adulthood and facing many decisions about their future. Deciding between college, marriage, or a career can create inner turmoil as they struggle with their identity as an adult. These add up to about all that a young person can handle—without adding the anxiety and trauma that a search for biological parents can entail.

I attended a meeting where a testimony was given by a twenty-one year old woman who had searched for her biological parents at a younger age and how it had affected her. She felt that she was now far more capable of coping with the issues involved than she was when she was younger. Another testimony given by a young woman who waited until she was twenty-one was very positive, and she had handled the situation well.

When an adopted child becomes a young adult, between nineteen and twenty-one depending on their maturity, the adoptive parents should share all the facts about their birth and be able to give him/her a letter written by the birth mother and/or birth father. This would help dispel some of the mystery of their past and give them a better understanding of their background.

The following letter was written by a birth mother and given to the adoptive parents to share with their daughter when she became a young woman.

To a very special girl:

By the time you read this letter, you will probably be a lovely young woman. But I wanted to let you know how much you mean to me and help you understand why I chose adoption.

I was almost nineteen when I learned that I was pregnant. At the time I wasn't getting along with my parents, so I moved in with my boyfriend (your father). But we soon realized that the relationship wasn't meant to be. Our love didn't last very long, and I moved back into my parents' house to find out in a few short weeks that I was pregnant. My friends advised me to have an abortion so everything would all be over. That way I wouldn't even have to tell my parents.

I thought about it, but abortion just didn't seem right. I had heard someone say that babies are formed even in a few weeks, so I decided to get counsel. After seeing films and materials, I decided that abortion was wrong and that it wasn't your fault that I got pregnant. You should be able to live and enjoy life.

Then I was faced with the problem of how to raise you. I wanted so badly to keep you and protect you, but I didn't have any financial support. Besides I wanted you to have a life with two parents to really care for you. So I looked into adoption. I loved you so much that I chose adoption so you could live a full and happy life.

If people could live on love alone, then maybe I could have raised you. But that's not reality. Maybe you don't understand right now, but I pray that someday you will. Every year on your birthday I try to imagine how you're growing into a lovely young woman. You will always hold a part of my heart. I will never forget you.

Love,

Your Birth Mother

This letter expresses a genuine love and concern for the child. Considering the circumstances, this birth mother tried to do what she felt was best for all concerned.

I would also like to share a letter written by a birth grand-mother. It gives insight into the feelings of other members of the family when a baby is given up for adoption.

Letter to an Unknown Grandchild

Dear One,

A year has passed since you began your life in this world. I still find many thoughts about you to be very painful, and I'll share some of them shortly. More and more, however, as time passes, I find myself thinking of you as a unique human being and a person in your own right. That's why I'm writing to you now.

When we finally faced the fact that your mother, my daughter, was carrying you, we had only a few months left to prepare for your arrival. For a long time, we had refused to deal with the problem before us. By the time you are old enough to read this, you will know that unmarried girls are not supposed to become pregnant. Because we are all human beings, facing many temptations in our lives and not always resisting them, we bring hardship upon ourselves.

Your mother and I found the help we knew we needed at a clinic near our home. It provided both physical and psychological help for pregnant teenagers and their families, either as inpatients or (as we chose) outpatients. Your mother attended prenatal classes, and later a kind and gentle doctor delivered you. A counselor helped your mother and our family deal with our feelings and emotions.

Your mother decided from the beginning to give you to adoptive parents so you could have the kind of home she could not provide. Although very young, she was wise enough to realize that she could not give you the security you deserved. She loved you enough to put your needs before her own.

An adoption agency found the parents just right for you. We can understand how thrilled they must have been to have you arrive at their home. Surely, it was all their Christmases and birthdays rolled into one little bundle.

"Little" is really the right word, too, because the agency we worked with believed in direct home placement. That is, instead of going to a foster home until your mother and father signed the final adoption papers, your adoptive parents took the chance that your biological parents would not change their minds and take you away from them. They had you with them as soon as you were ready to leave the hospital.

What peace and joy it gave us to know you were safe in their arms even though our own ached to hold you. No, we never did hold you, but we looked at you many, many times during your hospital stay; in fact, we have your picture tucked away in a drawer.

What a comfort it was to your grandma (and grandpa, too) to know that your mother had never considered abortion as a solution to her unplanned pregnancy. Our values in that regard are strong and can be summed up by the fact that everyone who advocates abortion has already been born. Accordingly, you, too, have now been born!

Finally, I should mention your father. A warm and gentle person, he supported your mother in all her decisions from the very beginning. When she was too frightened to turn to anyone else, he took her for medical care before we knew about the pregnancy. They believed they would always be together. But they are parted now, and only time will tell.

Oh, yes, and Grandpa. He doesn't talk about you a lot, but when he does, he always says one thing. That is, he hopes to be around if you should choose, when you are grown, to find your biological parents. The law has changed enough that it is possible. Since this is a very personal decision, we understand that it can only be made by the people involved at the proper time. May God guide you to make the right decision for you.

We wish you health, and a deep, abiding faith. With these, you will know happiness, and everything else will fall into place. We are sure that we are in your thoughts and prayers sometimes, as you will always remain in ours.

Love,

Grandma

What a blessing such a letter would be to an adopted child who is questioning his or her identity and sense of belonging. A sensitive letter like this could completely fulfill a child's need to know the circumstances that led to their adoption. You may want to suggest to the birth mother or other relatives that they write a letter expressing their feelings toward the child and the reason for their decision to give him or her up to be adopted.

The Right to Know?

It is still difficult today, if not impossible, for an adopted child to find out who their birth parents are. Adoptees seeking information on their birth records have faced obstacles in their attempts to bring about legislative changes.

Despite the fact that there were at least five million adoptees in the United States as of 1978,[1] they constitute a minority made up of white, black, foreign, and older adoptees. It has been difficult for these fragmented groups to identify with each other and work together. This is slowly changing, however.

Birth records started being automatically sealed in the 1940s. Only during the last few decades have a large number of adoptees become adults and begun to search for their roots. Adoptees who previously accepted sealed records began to question the "rules" as they saw other minority groups succeed by working together for freedom of choice. Some adoptees began to question what they felt was discrimination against their right to know their heritage.

Each individual adoption should be considered a unique circumstance, and the rights and needs of both the child and the birth parents should be prayerfully and sensitively weighed. Some birth parents welcome a reunion with the child as a second chance to tell their story about the love for the little one they gave up. Others fear the phone call or knock on the door that may bring their forgotten past rushing back into their lives.

Today there is much controversy over what exactly are the rights of the birth mother who placed her child for adoption with a guarantee of sealed records. One side says she relinquished her rights when she gave the child up. The other side says that her rights must be protected because she was promised that her secret would never be revealed.

One birth mother, in her fifties, finally had to face the day she could never prepare herself for. A phone call came from the daughter she had relinquished for adoption nearly forty years previously. The mother asked for time to explain this part of her past to her husband and family, and then the reunion was set. Mother and daughter both found they had nothing in common at this point in their lives other than a birth history. They parted with little contact thereafter. Still, a need had been met in both of them, and they were happy to part with positive feelings about each other.

Who Is Searching?

Studies have shown that the vast majority of adoptees will not find anything overwhelmingly negative in their past. An average profile of the information they will find is that they were illegitimate; the parents cared about each other but felt they could not provide a stable home for the child; the mother usually had the baby's welfare in mind in deciding upon adoption; and she remembers the child's birthday every year and wonders how he or she is doing.

The birth parents are generally found to be grateful to the adoptive parents for raising the adoptee, but most often they do not wish to suddenly become a participating parent at the time they are found. Often friendship, rather than relationship, results.

When one twenty-five-year-old, female adoptee was having difficulty getting pregnant, her doctor requested medical information on her mother and father to assist him with her problem. The young woman contacted the private agency that had placed her for adoption and was denied any information. Because of the medical need and with the full backing of her adoptive parents and an adoptee's support group, she was finally able to acquire her birth mother's name and her location.

As this young woman stood face to face with her unknown past, she became unsure of proceeding. Because she wanted to consider her birth mother's rights as well as her own, she faltered in her determination to find her.

Eventually she had a friend contact the birth mother, and the birth mother agreed to talk to the daughter by phone the following day. The birth mother acknowledged that she was her mother, but told her that she was married with a family who knew nothing of the adoption and she couldn't tell them. They have exchanged brief pieces of information and pictures from time to time, with the daughter hoping to convey that she is not seeking another family but only desiring to fill a missing link in her life.

The following facts were reported in *The Adoption Triangle*[2]:

1. Most adoptees who search are female.

2. Most reunions seem to be sought by adoptees who are told fairly late in life of their adoptions.

3. Most adoptees were satisfied with their reunions.

4. About half of the adoptees developed a meaningful relationship with the birth parents.

5. Searches for birth parents usually seem to be triggered by some significant event like the birth of a child or the death of the adoptive parent.

6. The adoptive family relationship was rarely damaged as a result of the reunion.

Some reunions between adoptees and their biological parents are highly fulfilling and provide the final piece to what the adoptee may feel was an incomplete puzzle in their background. A few reunions take place between adoptees and their birth fathers, but this is a rare occurrence.

Most adoptees really don't want a relationship with their birth parents; they are only curious about their background. One adoptee said, "I was adopted by two very beautiful people, and their love is priceless to me. But I sometimes wonder about my medical problem and where it came from."

As parents considering adoption, you will have to face this issue at some point. Ray and I feel it is best to resolve how you will deal with the situation before it arises. Set guidelines for yourselves and for the child. Then when questions arise, you and your spouse will be in agreement regarding how and when a search for the birth parent can begin.

If you have fears now, before adoption, ask the Lord to show you the source of your fear. You may be surprised that your anxiety over such a situation comes from insecurities deep within yourself. As you bring these to the Lord and ask Him to heal you, He will replace them with His perfect love and security. Then you will be free to welcome and receive a child who does not belong to you—but to the Lord.

And who knows—you may never be faced with the situation at all. One adopted child said, "I have never had any desire to know about my biological parents. I have no idea why I don't need to know—I just don't."

CHAPTER SEVENTEEN

The Perfect Family Planner

In the Larson home there are two children, a boy and a girl. Sounds like a well-planned family, and it was planned—but not by Rebecca and me. The plan for our family came straight from the heart of God.

We had always wanted a boy and a girl, two years apart. And after being married for five years, who could have designed it better? No one, except a loving heavenly Father who knows what is best for His children.

Every time we look at our two lovely adopted children, we realize anew that the Father knows best. Our need to raise children and our children's need to have both a father and mother are fulfilled. We believe it was a supernatural encounter ordered by God for these two children and this couple, Ray and Rebecca Larson, to be together in this life.

God can heal our infertility, even now, and make it possible for us to bear children. We know He is able, and we would rejoice to bring children into this world. But God has already given us a miracle—in a time when millions of children are being aborted and the number of children available for adoption is limited.

The miracle God worked in our lives stands as a testimony to God's love and faithfulness to everyone who knows us. Our children are *living* miracles because they were spared a tragic death in the womb. We would like to thank those mothers who had the courage to bear these two children and allow us to make them part of our family.

Although we cannot say "bone of my bone and flesh of my flesh," these children are *ours* in every other sense of the word.

In the spiritual realm, circumcision of the flesh could not complete the work of redemption. Instead, God's Word says we must have a circumcision of our heart in order to experience salvation through Jesus Christ. In the same way, children become ours through the work God does in our heart not by what happens in the flesh.

Because our son and daughter were relocated to our home by the working of the Holy Spirit, we feel a great responsibility in the rearing of these children. Our goal is to love them, minister to them, encourage them, strengthen them, and give them back to the Lord every day of our lives. It is the same as taking your own birth children, giving them back to the Lord, and promising to raise them up as He requires.

We are confident that God has a specific and perfect plan for our children, and we are thankful to have a part in the development of the destiny of two spiritual lives who are going to be mightily used by God.

How God Answers Prayer

God's Word says, "He settles the barren woman in her home as a happy mother of children" (Psalm 113:9). That is the promise. *How* God brings children into the home is His decision. Yet, whatever God chooses will be best for the parents and the children and not necessarily according to our specified request.

Many of the blessings and supernatural workings of God would have been lost if I had insisted that God answer my prayer *my way*. Thankfully, God doesn't always answer our prayers immediately or give us His complete plan all at once. We couldn't handle it, and we'd probably muddle everything with our selfish, willful interference.

God can answer *your* prayer for children in two ways. He can heal your infertility and make it possible for you to give birth to natural children. Or, He can make a way for you to adopt a child. Both are beautiful and miraculous events that will allow God to be glorified in your life and family.

God's Word declares, "Delight yourself in the Lord and he will give you the desires of your heart" (Psalm 37:4). Our desire for children was fulfilled—in God's time and in His way.

The Father heart of God wants to supply all of our needs, to bless us, and to show us His reliability and character. But the crucial question becomes, Are *we* doing the will of God as He prescribes in the Word? Or, are we trying to work things out in our own understanding?

The book of Proverbs says, "Trust in the Lord with all your heart and lean not on your own understanding; in all your ways acknowledge him, and he will make your paths straight" (3:5,6). We put our trust in God, and He directed our every step.

Our Father really does know best. Let's learn to trust Him to bring about our highest good in every situation. Successful living comes from relying upon His reliability.

A High Risk Venture

Adoption is a high risk venture—both financially and emotionally. But Rebecca and I soon discovered that the real issue was not the risks involved—it was whether we would be obedient to God or not. "Without faith it is impossible to please God" (Hebrews 11:6). *Faith* is obeying God in spite of the risks.

Hebrews 11:11 says, "Through faith also Sarah herself received strength to conceive seed and was delivered of a child when she was past age. Because she judged him faithful who had promised" (KJV).

Just as Sarah believed God was faithful, so did we. Through faith we took financial steps that many would say were unwise because of the risks involved in an independent adoption. Through faith we went ahead with an agency adoption when we had already been disappointed in an earlier encounter. But God had promised us, and we had to stand on the reliability of our Father God to do what is best for us and our children.

Oh, there were rough times, but those stones in the pathway created faith and confidence in the Father heart of God that we might never have learned otherwise. In fact, there are still times when we struggle with not being able to bear our own children. Yet, in our hearts we know that God's plan is perfect and without flaw.

Most of us want a smooth pathway with no obstacles or bumps. Such a pleasant ride, however, does not develop character or faith. His goal is for us to be effective ministers for His Kingdom in everything we do and say. God wants to conform us to the image of Jesus Christ to enable us to serve Him and to share His life with others.

When we face obstacles and are obedient to Him, we are made aware of God's ability to intervene and take care of any potential problem in our lives. That increases our faith in God and in His wonder-working power.

Rebecca and I have grown through our experiences with infertility and adoption. God has used the grief, the embarrassment, the frustration, and the miracles to mold our character and strengthen our faith. We have learned that God is capable, reliable, and willing to meet our needs.

Stand on the Promises

Our story is miraculous, but it is not meant to be one in a million. Remember, no matter what your situation, God wants to help you gain the victory. You may have chosen to remain a couple without children; or you may believe God has promised physical healing; or you may be waiting to adopt. Perhaps you aren't sure how God will answer your prayer for children. But if you combat unbelief and stand against the enemy, victory will come.

I cannot tell you how many times the devil came against Rebecca and me, trying to condemn us and make us feel inferior and cheated. He continued to try to confuse the situation by sending signals contradictory to God's Word.

The Bible says, "The weapons we fight with are not the weapons of the world. On the contrary, they have divine power to demolish strongholds" (2 Corinthians 10:4). We must pull down every idea and thought that exalts itself against the knowledge of God.

Bring every negative thought under the control of the Holy Spirit. Don't allow Satan's fiery darts to catch fire in your mind. Refuse to dwell on your doubts, fears, and frustrations. When you are struggling, remember that He knows your hurt better than you do. Jesus bore your grief and carried your sorrow. (See Isaiah 53:4.) Nothing we could face is greater than what He has faced for us.

We recommend that you memorize Scripture, particularly about children and childbirth. Become familiar with all the miracles that God did in the lives of childless couples in the Bible.

At the same time, get help from others. Don't do it alone. Remember, "Many advisers make victory sure" (Proverbs 11:14).

Seek out godly counselors for help and advice. When you are battling feelings of failure, contact people who have gone through a similar situation or who have the faith and understanding to help you. Seek every possible means of encouragement, wisdom, and support.

If God has promised you a healing, memorize James 5:14,15. These verses say that the Lord will heal those who ask the elders of the church to pray for them. If you humble yourself before God's servants and request prayer, the Lord has promised to touch you. God can and does heal infertility problems.

We have prayed for many couples who have conceived and given birth to children. One couple was told by their doctor that they had very little chance of having children. During a church service a word of knowledge was spoken, telling them that they would conceive and give birth to children of their own. Two weeks later the wife was found to be pregnant.

On several occasions in our ministry I have sensed the need to declare that God was healing a barren woman. The proof of the healing became evident when the woman delivered a healthy child and gave all the glory to God.

Jesus promised us abundant life—a full, complete, rewarding life. No English word quite parallels the word Jesus used in the original language. Our lives are to be rich, full, and promising. For each individual, God has a unique and beautiful way of supplying the blessings that will make our life abundant in every sense of the word.

The Bible says that it has not even entered into the mind of man what the Father heart of God has conceived for His children. What a great promise! When we stand on God's

Word and His promises, we have the confidence to defeat the enemy and rise above negative circumstances in our lives.

When the Womb is Empty

Rebecca and I wrote this book to supply you with the ways and means to help you deal with your infertility successfully. We also wanted to address the issue of adoption from a Christian perspective. We believe that God can and will intervene in your life to bring about His highest good for you. Not just because you ask but because He loves you and has a perfect plan for you and your family.

Some of you will miraculously bear children. Many of you will adopt. Some will both adopt and bear children. A few of you will decide that it is not in God's perfect plan for you to be used as parents.

Regardless of the outcome, God wants His peace to rule your heart. He will confirm His will with miraculous circumstances and details that will let you know beyond the shadow of a doubt that He loves you and has only your best interests at heart.

Before the foundation of the world, God had in mind a plan that would enable us to spend eternity with Him. He sent His very own Son to die on a cross. There is no doubt in our minds that all His ways are perfect and motivated only by love.

Put your faith in the Lord Jesus Christ, and allow Him to bring about His perfect and beautiful plan for your life. Fix your eyes on Jesus, the author and perfecter of your faith. Trust in Him, love Him, and minister to others. You will be amazed at how He will demonstrate that He is the perfect family planner, even *when the womb is empty*.

Notes

CHAPTER THREE

1. *Newsweek,* December 6, 1982, pp. 32-33,40,43, "Infertility—New Cures, New Hopes."
2. *Women's Day,* May 22, 1984, p. 32, "New Hope For Troubled Couples."
3. *Newsweek*
4. *Woman's Day*
5. *Newsweek*
6. *Prevention Magazine,* April, 1981, pp. 91-93, "Infertility Was Our Problem."

CHAPTER FIVE

1. *Charisma,* September, 1987, p. 43.

CHAPTER SIXTEEN

1. J. W. Small, "Discrimination Against the Adoptee," *Public Welfare,* Vol. 37, 1979, pp.38-43.
2. A. D. Sorosky, et al., *The Adoption Triangle: The Effects of the Sealed Records on Adoptees, Birth Parents, and Adoptive Parents* (Garden City, New York: Anchor Press, 1978).

APPENDIX I

Strategies for Pro-Life Activism

Rebecca has compiled a list of ways you can help fight against the holocaust of abortion. Read through this list and let the Lord guide concerning ways you can get actively involved both on a personal level and with pro-life organizations. Our prayer is that you, as an infertile couple, will be found on the front lines of this battle to save the unborn.

Pray.
—Ask God to quickly put an end to the ongoing holocaust of abortion.
—Intercede for innocent babies in the womb and the young women considering abortion.
—Pray that government lawmakers will either have a change of heart regarding abortion legislation or that God will replace them with pro-life candidates.

Be informed.
—Know what abortion really is and the different procedures used to abort a baby.
—Obtain information from pro-life organizations or write to: *Last Days Ministries, Box 40, Lindale, Texas 75771.* Their tracts, "Children—Things We Throw Away" and "The Questions Most People Ask About Abortion", are excellent.

—Memorize statistics regarding the number of abortions performed, etc.
—Know the side-effects and long-term results that an abortion can have on a woman.

Keep abreast of legislation affecting the abortion issue.

—Know the facts. Become informed about the legal aspects surrounding abortion.
—Read detailed information regarding human life issues.
—Keep abreast of state and local statistics and legislation.
—Support a human life amendment to the constitution that will protect the unborn.

Support pro-life organizations.

—Contact pro-life groups and ask them to put your name on their mailing list.
—Contribute financially to the organization.
—Volunteer your time speaking, doing office work, counseling, distributing literature, or whatever your talents may be.
—If there is no pro-life group in your area, start one.

Help girls/women with unwanted pregnancies.

—Encourage unwed pregnant girls to carry their babies full-term and to put them up for adoption or to keep them.
—Open your home to them.
—Give financial aid if needed.
—Get involved in a local crisis pregnancy hot-line program. This will enable you to receive valuable counseling training and material.
—Support homes for unwed mothers.

Inform others.
—Take every opportunity to speak out and let your views be known.
—Make other Christians and your church aware of the facts.
—Ask your pastor to help promote pro-life seminars in your church.
—Help organize a pro-life rally in your church or city. Invite pastors, doctors, and other local leaders to take a public stand against abortion.
—Show pro-life films in churches, schools, etc.

Do sidewalk counseling at abortion clinics.
—Many pregnant women don't know that other options are available, and many of them feel pressed into making a quick decision. Your sincere counsel at this crisis point could be a matter of life and death for the child they are carrying.
—Let her know that you care and that you are there to help her. God hates abortion but loves the pregnant woman.
—Be willing to financially help a girl or take her into your home.
—Pass out leaflets with pictures of aborted babies. Many women have no idea of what abortion really is and the pain that an unborn aborted baby faces. A picture is worth a thousand words.

Use the media to awaken public consciousness.
—Sponsor a billboard.
—Run an ad in your daily newspaper and other papers.
—Purchase air time on the radio. The cost may be less than you think. Write to *Minnesota Citizens Concerned for Life, 4249 Nicollet Avenue, Minneapolis, Minnesota 55409* for more information.

Take the pro-life message to your community.
—Attend and speak at city council, school board, and other civic meetings.
—Show films and slide presentations to youth groups, churches, schools, garden clubs, civic organizations, etc. You must go to them, they won't come to you. Films can also be rented or purchased from *American Portrait Film, 1695 West Crescent Avenue, Suite 500, Anaheim, CA 92801; 714-535-2189*

Take the pro-life message into the schools.
—Ask Christian teachers or students to speak on the abortion issue to a class or a student assembly. Most young people are unaware of the facts about abortion and are potential abortion customers.
—Distribute pro-life literature to students.
—Start a pro-life group on high school and college campuses. Teenagers who know the truth can make their peers aware of what abortion really is and the dangers involved in having one.
—Find out whether Planned Parenthood operates in your high schools. If they do, go to the principal and ask for equal time to present the other side of the story. This may take persistence, but it's worth it if one baby is saved.
—Donate pro-life books to high school and college libraries. Write to *Minnesota Citizens Concerned for Life, 4249 Nicollet Avenue, Minneapolis, MN 55409* and ask for their Directory of Pro-Life Information.

Contact local physicians by phone or letter.
—Urge them not to perform abortions.
—Ask them to carry pro-life literature in their waiting rooms.
—Don't support doctors who perform abortions.
—Encourage those who are against abortion to take a stand.

Get involved during election campaigns.
—Register to vote.
—Become actively involved in the political campaigns of pro-life candidates.
—Find out how candidates feel about abortion, and don't vote for them if they won't tell you.
—Obtain a list of pro-life candidates from you local right-to-life organization.
—Find out how candidates have voted on past abortion laws.

Distribute pro-life literature.
—Blitz your city. It is illegal to put tracts in mail boxes, but it's okay to slip them under a door or affix them to a door knob. To obtain flyers and tracts contact: *Heritage House, P.O. Box 730, Taylor, AZ 85959; 602-536-7592.*
—Distribute pro-life literature in public places, city sidewalks, malls, shopping areas, fairgrounds, etc.

Picket abortion clinics and the offices of doctors who perform abortions.
—Don't picket alone. Join a particular pro-life group and follow their guidelines. Picketing brings the whole issue of abortion to public attention. Most doctors don't want people to know they perform abortions.
—Count the cost and realize you will have opposition. As long as you picket legally, your right to picket is protected by the First Amendment.
—Write to *Operation Rescue, P.O. Box 1180, Binghamton, New York 13901* for information on Christ-centered, peaceful demonstrations.

Write to your senators and congressmen.
—You have every right to voice your opinion because they are your representatives. Each letter from a constituent is

considered to represent the opinion of several thousand voters.

—To find the addresses of your state senators and representatives look in the section for government offices in the telephone book. Your U.S. senators and representatives will also be in the government section listed under "United States."

How to write an effective letter to your representatives.

—Be brief and to the point. A brief letter that gets to the point of the matter will receive much more attention than a long, detailed one in which your message is lost.

—Write legibly. Handwritten letters are fine if they are readable.

—Make your letters personal. Each letter should be individualized and written in your own words. Duplicated form letters and postcards never have the impact that a personalized letter does.

—Be positive and constructive. Avoid criticism.

—Compliment your legislator on some recent action, vote, or speech. Appreciation is seldom given and much is needed by these men and women.

—Never be rude or threatening. Some people act as though the normal rules of courtesy do not apply to politicians. Be sure not to attack the member's staff, even indirectly, by such comments as, "I hope this gets past your secretary." You need the staff on your side or, at least, not actively against you. Do not threaten that you will campaign against the legislators at the next election. Threats are resented, and they already know that letter writers are active in politics.

—Be persistent. Don't be put off by a negative answer from your legislator. Write again; this lets them know you are serious. Get others to write. A flood of mail can often influence a politician to change his mind or at least reconsider a certain issue.

What to include in your letter.
—Write in a way that shows you understand the "pros" and "cons" of the specific issue they are considering. Keep stressing the local impact of the issue; this is what concerns your congressman the most.
—Find the number of abortions done last year in your city or congressional district or state.
—Tell your congressman about malpractice suits against local abortionists.
—Include incidents regarding local women who were pressured into having abortions.
—Include favorable pro-life articles and editorials from local papers.
—Within the text of your letter, ask a thoughtful question about the pro-life issue that will require a response from your legislator. Otherwise, you'll probably only receive a form letter in reply.
—Tell them you are in favor of a human life amendment to the Constitution that could overturn the Supreme Court decision of 1973.

APPENDIX II

Agency Adoption Forms

Before a couple is accepted by an agency, several forms must be completed along with an autobiography of each prospective parent. Using different types of forms, we have compiled a list of sample questions and information needed.

Family History Sheet:

—Name, birthdate, address, religion.
—Physical description: Hair, eyes, complexion, height, weight, national background.
—Applicant's Father: Residence, age, education, occupation, church, death: date/cause.
—Applicant's Mother (same information as above).
—Applicant's Siblings (same information as above).
—Family characteristics (essay answer).
—Areas where your family or friends reside or have strong ties (essay answer).
—Health: Several physical conditions and illnesses are listed on the form to be checked off if applicable. Other illnesses (physical/mental) are to be described.

Personal Questionnaire:
(Husband and wife to fill out individual forms)

1. Describe your personality.
2. Describe your spouse's personality.
3. If you have any children, describe them.
4. Your Marriage:
   a. What are your main areas of disagreement?
   b. What are the areas in which you agree on childrearing?
   c. Do you and your spouse feel the same about adopting? How did you come to consider adopting?
   d. What is your yearly income? What are your priorities when you spend money? Do you and your spouse agree on this?
5. What are your common interests and things you do as a family?
6. What strengths do you have as a person that will help you to parent?
7. What goals would you set for your children in your home?
8. What are your preferences for a child? Include number of children desired, age range, sex, race background, temperament, and behavior.
9. What kind of child would you prefer not to parent?

How to Write an Autobiography

Husband and wife must each complete their own autobiography. Each agency will have different guidelines for writing your autobiography, and some supply a form with answers to be filled in. Below is a list of questions and ideas compiled from several different forms. This will give you an idea of the kinds of questions you can expect to answer.

Agencies suggest that you emphasize your feelings and reactions to people and events rather than details surrounding the circumstances. Try to respond to each question or issue with as much information as you can remember without worrying about your answers being too long. Also, any other important events or areas of your life not suggested should be included.

A. Your Family:

Parents:
Describe your parents as a couple.
Their marriage during your childhood.
Areas of agreement and disagreement.
How major issues (money, sex education, discipline, punishment, etc.) were handled.
What kind of relationship existed between mother and father?
Father's name, age, education, occupation.
His personality and relationship with the children.
Sibling most like father and father's favorite.
Mother's name, age, education, occupation.
Her personality and relationship with the children.
Sibling most like mother and mother's favorite.
Who were you closer to?
How were you raised, disciplined, etc.
As a parent, what would you do similar or dissimilar.

Siblings:
Number of children in your family of origin.
Birth order and age differences.
Who in your family you felt closest to and why.
What was your relationship with your family members?

B. Childhood and Youth:

Describe the home, neighborhood, and community in which you grew up.

What were you like a kid (describe your personality).

How did you spend your time?

Who were your friends?

What are your most pleasant memories, your unhappy memories?

How did you feel about school? How far did you go with your education?

What were your favorite subjects?

What were your special talents or interests?

Include the most and least enjoyable aspects of your education as well as any experiences that were rewarding or disappointing.

Most important problems/concerns during teens; areas of special interest.

Religious orientation.

What made you happy/angry?

Dating experiences, etc.

Describe your most significant experiences growing up.

Who were the most important people in your childhood/your youth? What kind of influence did they have on you?

C. Courtship and Marriage:

How did you meet your spouse? What attracted you to him/her?

What common interests do you and your spouse share?

How and why did you decide to marry?

Changes in your relationship after the honeymoon period.

How do you settle differences of opinion or disagreements with each other?

Describe your spouse today.

Describe yourself today.

Your mutual interests and separate interests.

Your strengths you bring to the marriage.

Areas of disagreement.

Who manages the money in your family?

How are financial decisions made?

What are your relationships with each other's families? Do they live within visiting distance? When do you get together?

What are the similarities and dissimilarities between families?

How do your families feel about your adopting?

Problems in your marriage that you have overcome. Tell how you worked them out.

If possible, what would you change about your marriage and how would you change it?

Any previous marriage: Brief outline of situation leading to the marriage and its dissolution.

D. Children:

What is your experience with children?

What age children do you enjoy being with most?

What are your methods of discipline with children? How do you set limits? How did you arrive at this?

For those who have a child or children:

Describe each child physically along with a personality sketch.

What are your child's or children's attitudes toward adopting a baby or another child.

Describe your relationship with your child.

For those who do not have children:
Describe your philosophy of childrearing, discipline, and punishment.

E. Adoption:

When did you start thinking about adoption and why?

What are your reason(s) for wanting to adopt a child?

If you have had infertility testing, what were the results and how do you feel about them?

If you want a foreign or special needs child, tell why.

What type of child do you wish to adopt?

What can you offer a child?

What do you expect from a child?

How you anticipate a child will fit into your family.

Do you have family or friends who have adopted?

Do you know anyone who has released her child for adoptive planning?

Are you or do you plan to get involved in a local adoptive support group?

F. Your interests:

What kind of work do you do? How do you feel about the way you spend your days? Do you have hopes or plans for change in your daily routine?

What do you do for relaxation and fun?

Describe individual interests, shared interests, and organizations you belong to.

Who are the people you socialize with?

How would an adopted child fit into some of your social activities?

How do you expect life will change with the addition of a child or children?

What are your skills and capacities? In what areas would you like to develop?

G. Employment:

Describe your job. For those who do not work outside the home, comment on previous employment and how you feel about your current situation.

Your position and duties.

Kind of business or profession.

Special training and/or expertise.

How did you develop to get to this position?

How do you feel about your work (or in-home situation)?

Satisfactions/dissatisfactions of your work (or in-home situation).

Future goals.

H. Home and Community.

Describe your house, size, number of rooms, property/grounds.

Describe your neighborhood, and community.

What community resources are available to you?

How do you think an adopted child will be accepted in your neighborhood?

What kind of school will your child attend?

In making your decision to adopt, describe the reaction and degree of support from parents, relatives, friends, church family.

I. Religion:

Describe your faith when growing up.
What is the importance of religion in your life?
Current church membership and or activities.
Your attitudes toward religion.

J. General:

Describe the strongest influence in your life.
Your greatest personal achievement.
Your greatest personal disappointment.
Difficulties you've faced, your method of coping, and what you learned for and about yourself.
Your current goals in life.
Is there anything about your life you would like to change (exclude plans for adoption) and if so, what and why.
Health of family members.
Health problems or concerns.
Any additional comments about any part of your life or self not covered in this outline.

Adoptive Placement Agreement

Once the child is placed in your home, and before the adoption is finalized, an agreement similar to the one below must be signed. The agency remains as legal guardian of the child until adoption is final.

We, _____ and _____ under-
    (Adoptive Father)   (Adoptive Mother)
stand that _____ Adoption Agency, in accepting us as adoptive parents expresses confidence in our ability to meet the needs of the child placed with us on _____. Having
           (date of placement)
seen the child and been informed of his/her social and health history, we accept him/her with the intent of legal adoption. We understand that the Agency holds legal custody of the child until the adoption is completed in court or until an interlocutory decree of adoption is granted. We understand that the social worker, prior to the completion of adoption, including the period an interlocutory decree of adoption is in effect, will visit us and the child regularly, until the adoption is final.

We agree to place the child under the care of a physician and follow recommendations for health care for the child, including immunization. We shall notify the Agency of any serious illnesses of the child. However, we understand that we are authorized to permit medical and surgical care which may be necessary.

We agree to inform the Agency of changes in our family or place of residence. We shall not take the child out of the state without the Agency's consent, unless an interlocutory decree of adoption is in effect, and we agree to inform the Agency of extended trips taken outside our county of residence.

If for any reason we cannot keep the child or properly care for him/her, we shall ask the Agency to make other arrangements for the child. If, before the adoption is completed, we are dissatisfied with a decision affecting the placement of the child in our home, we have the right to request a grievance review. We understand that if there is no interlocutory decree of adoption in effect the Agency may remove the child immediately if the child is endangered or upon seven (7) days notice if it is determined that such action will be for the best interest of the child. If an interlocutory decree is granted, the child can only be removed by court approval or a child protective service action. In such event, we do hereby waive and release any and all claims we may have against the Agency for board, lodging, maintenance, and care of the child, and for any damages resulting therefrom.

We understand that we are responsible for any attorney fees incurred in completing the adoption.

We have been informed of the provisions of the Adoption Assistance Program (AAP) to assist in the placement of special needs children. . . . We understand that we may receive AAP benefits only if an

Adoption Assistance Agreement is completed prior to a final decree of adoption.

In consideration of services rendered to us we agree to pay to the Agency the balance due of the adoption fee by the time the agency recommends the adoption in its report to the court.

The above agreement is signed by both parents and the agency representatives.

The following Placement Affidavit is also completed at the time the child is placed with the adoptive parents.

To Whom It May Concern:

This statement is to confirm that _____ born on _____ was placed in the home of _____ on _____ for the purpose of adoption. Hereafter, these adoptive parents assume full responsibility for this child.

This placement was made by _____ Adoption Agency, a licensed home-finding and adoption agency in the state of _____.

In view of the authority given to the Agency, these adoptive parents are hereby authorized to give permission for medical and surgical care which may be needed by this child. This authorization is given them until such time as the final decree of adoption is issued by the court.

This form is signed by the agency caseworker.

APPENDIX III

Resume Guidelines for Independent Adoption

The following outline shows you how to set up an adoption letter to use along with your resume. The sample cover letter will assist you in tailoring ones for yourselves.

Cover Letter

General Layout Ideas

Use beige or off-white paper, avoid pure white or bright colors.

Simple textured paper is best.

Have the resume printed, avoid photocopies.

One 8 1/2 x 11 sheet each for resume and cover letter.

Have several hundred copies printed.

Have matching envelopes printed.

Put your name in bold letters.

Use a decorative border or good graphics, if possible.

Put your own personalities into the letter and resume.

Make it short and simple.

Letter

Print your cover letter on same paper as the resume.

A computer is helpful in personalizing each letter.

Put your address on left side.

Salutation should read: To Whom It May Concern.
Include a short introduction.
Briefly explain infertility.
Give brief description of child that you are looking for such as: age, sex, health, racial background.
If you want to consider handicapped children, explain the degree of handicap you feel you can care for—whether semi, major, or profound.
Give permission to call twenty-four hours a day.
Give your home phone, work phones, attorney's phone, relative's phone. Make sure you include area code and permission to call collect.
Close the letter by thanking them for their time and consideration.
Sign the letter personally with both your signatures.

Envelope

Business size.
Same color and texture as resume and cover letter.
Have return address printed to match resume and cover letter.
When sent out, type address neatly (try to match same print as return address).
No stick-on labels or rubber stamps for return address.

Sample Letter

Date
Your Name
Your Address

To Whom It May Concern:

We are writing to you in hopes that you may be able to assist us in our pursuit of private adoption. After extensive testing for infertility, we have exhausted any hope of having children ourselves.

My husband and I are both in our late twenties and have been happily married for seven years. We enjoy traveling and spending our spare time just being together. We have a very close relationship, but one very important ingredient is missing—a child to raise and share our lives and love with.

We live in a nice community sixty miles north of San Francisco. Both of us grew up in a small town, and we would like to raise our children in the same type of quiet, country setting. We have owned our home for five years. It has three bedrooms and a big, fenced backyard. We have made many improvements preparing for our family.

We are both born again Christians and are actively involved in our local church. Teaching Sunday school, singing in the choir, and working with the teens give us opportunities to share the joy of Christ with others.

My husband has worked seven years with a local tile distributing company and likes his work. He just recently was promoted to a managerial position. He enjoys many outdoor activities such as golf, skiing, and camping.

I have worked six years for a local credit union, although I am anxiously looking forward to staying home to raise a long awaited child. Cooking, crocheting, embroidering, and homemaking are things I especially like to do.

We are interested in adopting a Caucasian child, birth to three years old, male or female, from corrective handicap to excellent health.

We deeply desire to have a child to complete our family. If you know of one who is in need of a good home and loving parents, please contact us immediately. You can write us or call *collect* evenings (home area code and phone number) or days *collect* at (work area code and phone number).

On behalf of our parents and families, we would like to thank you for your kind attention and consideration of this very special request.

Sincerely,

(personal signature)   (personal signature)
   Husband's name   Wife's name

Resume

A well-designed resume will help the prospective birth mother or her contact to immediately form a positive opinion of you. Try to be as informative as possible. Here are some specific guidelines and a sample for you to follow.

General Outline

Include name, address, phone numbers (as suggested above).

Attach photo of your family (as they currently appear) on right side of resume.

Use short phrases with only positive, expressive words.
Include family statistics:
   Date of marriage
   Home ownership
   Family interests and hobbies
Personal statistics (for each individual—husband, wife, other children if any):
   Birthdates
   Denomination or Church affiliation
   Health
   Racial background
   Education
   Personality

Occupation
Appearance

Financial statistics:
Income range
Homeowner (describe home)

Sample Resume

Mr. and Mrs. John Smith
111 Dream Lane
Hopewell, CA
Home phone (222) 121-3333
Work phone (222) 121-4444 John's
Work phone (222) 121-5555 Mary's

Family Statistics

Married: April 2, 1978

Interests: Husband—Enjoys all sports, but particu-
               larly skiing, racquetball and basketball.
               Loves speaking to groups and writing.
               Wife:—Enjoys all crafts, gardening, aero-
               bics, sewing, sports and working with
               children.
               Together—We love to camp, participate
               in sports, refinish furniture, and spend a
               lot of quality time together each week as
               a family.

Church: Faith Community Church

Personal Statistics

Husband's name:	John Smith
Born:	September 8, 1953, in Huntington Beach, California.
Health:	Excellent.
Education:	Degree from USC in Business Administration.
Nationality:	German.
Personality:	Outgoing, fun loving, and amiable.
Appearance:	Brown hair and blue eyes with olive complexion. Height: 6' Weight: 160 lbs.
Occupation:	Supervises accounting department for a manufacturing company.

Wife's name:	Mary Smith
Born:	October 24, 1958, in Phoenix, Arizona.
Health:	Good. Has slight hearing loss in left ear.
Education:	Degree from USC in Elementary Education.
Nationality:	Dutch and Norwegian.
Personality:	Soft-spoken and gentle but effervescent.
Appearance:	Dark blond hair, blue-green eyes, fair complexion. Height: 5'7" Weight: 115 lbs.
Occupation:	First priority is being a mother and housewife. Also actively involved in teaching Sunday school and children's choir. Director of women's ministries at her church.

Financial Statistics

Earnings: $30,000-40,000 per year
Life
Insurance: $150,000
Home: New, 3 bedroom, 2 bath on 1/8 acre lot.
Equity: $10,000

Photograph

Including a recent photograph along with your resume and cover letter adds a personal touch and gives the prospective birth mother or contact an immediate impression of you as a couple or family. Follow these guidelines for making a good first impression:

Photo should be professional and convey warmth.
Should be no larger than 3 1/2 x 4 1/2 to fit in upper right hand corner of resume.
Use color.
Only one photo per resume.
No Polaroid prints.
Wear soft, warm colors.
Choose a simple, uncluttered background.
Your present family should be in the picture.
Picture should be recent.
Make sure that the placement of the photo does not interfere with the folding of the resume when it is placed in the envelope.
Use double-stick tape on back of photo to keep everything neat.

Where to Send Resumes

Sending personal and private information to complete strangers seems risky, especially in this day and age. But it is necessary in order to make contact with people who may be able to lead you to the right birth mother. You may want to be selective at first and then branch out if your responses are limited in the beginning. Here are some ideas of people and places you may want to send your resume.

Attorneys
Churches
Pastors
Friends
Parent adoption support groups
Pro-life groups
Organizations that specialize in independent adoptions
Doctors (pro-life, gynecologists, obstetricians) inside and outside your state. (You can get list of doctors from some hospitals or libraries.)
School nurses and guidance counselors at local high schools, junior highs, colleges, or universities
Send out in Christmas cards. (I know of some couples who had success with this.)
To anyone you know—nurses, pharmacists, Avon lady, insurance man, postman, etc.

APPENDIX IV

Adoption Agencies

Domestic, Foreign, and Hard to Place Children

Tracking down all the private agencies and placement centers in your state will require some research on your part. You may want to start with your local telephone book. Your county and state offices should be listed in the Guide to Human Services section of the phone book under "Adoption" or "Community Services" or "Social Services" or "County Children's Bureau." Some private agencies are listed in the yellow pages under "Adoption Services."

Several church denominations have children's homes and/or offer adoption services. Catholic Charities and Catholic Social Services are quite active in placing special needs children. Lutheran Social Services has been a pioneer in this area as well. There are Baptist, Methodist, and Presbyterian children's homes throughout the nation, offering services to people of all denominations.

You can obtain general adoption information, resource materials, and a list of licensed agencies in each state from:

National Adoption Center
1218 Chestnut Street
Philadelphia, Pennsylvania 19107
215-925-0200

Our state by state list contains the member agencies of The National Committee for Adoption. For more information you may want to purchase their excellent publication called *Adoption Factbook: United States Data, Issues, Regulations and Resources*. It is available from their office. Write to:

National Committee for Adoption
2025 M Street N.W.
Washington, D.C. 20036
202-463-7559

Our list also includes all the offices of Bethany Christian Services available at this time. Satellite offices open frequently, so you will want to write or phone the national headquarters for an updated list. Write to:

Bethany Christian Services
901 Eastern Avenue N.E.
Grand Rapids, Michigan 49503
616-459-6273 or 800-BETHANY

The Adoption Resource Book by Lois Gilman contains a very thorough listing of state and private agencies as well as contacts for intercountry and special needs adoptions. Your local bookstore should be able to order one for you. It is published by Harper and Row with a revised edition released in 1987.

In the list of adoption agencies below, the first listing for each state is the State Agency. They can provide information regarding your state's specific regulations and laws regarding adoption and put you in contact with the city or county agency nearest you.

Some of the private agencies listed serve several states or have branch offices in other cities. You may also want to contact agencies in neighboring states.

State and Private Adoption Agencies

ALABAMA

State Department of Human Resources
64 North Union Street
Montgomery, AL 36130
205-261-3409

AGAPE (Association for Guidance, Aid,
Placement, & Empathy)
2733 Mastin Lake Road
Huntsville, AL 35810
205-859-4481

Lifeline Children's Services
2908 Pump House Road
Birmingham, AL 35243
205-967-0811

ALASKA

Alaska Department of Health and Social Services
Pouch H-05
Juneau, AK 99811
907-465-3631

ARIZONA

Arizona Department of Economic Security
1400 West Washington
Phoenix, AZ 85009
602-255-3981

Christian Family Care Agency
1105 East Missouri
Phoenix, AZ 85014
602-264-9891

House of Samuel
11777 South Old Nogales Highway
Tucson, AZ 85706
602-294-1997

ARKANSAS

Department of Human Services
P.O. Box 1437
Little Rock, AR 72207
501-371-2207

Bethany Christian Services
Prospect Building, Suite 564
1501 North University
Little Rock, AR 72207-5242
501-664-5729

CALIFORNIA

Adoptions Branch
Department of Social Services
744 P Street
Sacramento, CA 95814
916-322-5973

Bethany Christian Services
1150 Mark Randy Place
Modesto, CA 95350
209-522-5121

Bethany Christian Services
9556 Flower #1
Bellflower, CA 90706
213-804-3448

Children's Home Society of California
2727 West 6th Street
Los Angeles, CA 90057
213-482-5443

Christian Adoption & Family Services
2121 West Crescent, Suite 106
Anaheim, CA 92801
213-860-3766

Vista Del Mar Child-Care Service
3200 Motor Avenue
Los Angeles, CA 90034
213-836-1223

COLORADO

Department of Social Services
717 Seventeenth Street
Denver, CO 80218-0899
303-294-5962

Bethany Christian Services
2140 South Ivanhoe, Suite 106
Denver, CO 80222
303-758-4484

CONNECTICUT

Connecticut Adoption Resource Exchange
176 Sigourney Street
Hartford, CT 06105
203-566-8742

Family Life Center
79 Birch Hill
Weston, CT 06833
203-222-1468

DELAWARE

Adoption Services Coordinator
Division of Child Protective Services
330 East 30th Street
Wilmington, DE 19802
302-571-6419

DISTRICT OF COLUMBIA

Department of Human Services
500 First Street N.W.
Washington, D.C. 20001
202-727-3161

Adoption Services Information Agency/ASIA
7720 Alaska Avenue N.W.
Washington, D.C. 20012
202-726-7193

Barker Foundation
4545 42nd Street N.W., Suite 207
Washington, D.C. 20016
202-363-7751

FLORIDA

Department of Health & Rehabilitation Services
1317 Winewood Boulevard
Tallahassee, FL 32301
904-488-8000

Mt. Dora Christian Home & Bible School
P.O. Box 896
Mt. Dora, FL 32757
904-383-2155

Shepherd Care Ministries
925 Taft Street, Suite B
Hollywood, FL 33021
305-981-2060

GEORGIA

Georgia Department of Human Resources
878 Peachtree Street N.E.
Atlanta, GA 30309
404-894-4456

In His Care Harvester Human Services
4650 Flat Shoals Road
Decatur, GA 30034
404-243-5112

Open Door Adoption Agency
323A East Jackson Street
Thomasville, GA 31799-0004
912-228-6339

HAWAII

Department of Social Services
1149 Bethel Street
Honolulu, HI 96813
808-548-6739

IDAHO

Department of Health and Welfare
450 North State
Boise, ID 83720
208-334-3546

Christian Counseling Services
545 Shoup Avenue
Idaho Falls, ID 83402
208-529-4673

ILLINOIS

Adoption Information Center of Illinois
201 North Wells Street, Suite 1342
Chicago, IL 60606
312-346-1516

Bethany Christian Services
9730 South Western Street, Suite 203
Evergreen Park, IL 60642
312-422-9626

The Cradle Society
2049 Ridge Avenue
Evanston, IL 60204
312-475-5800

Evangelical Child & Family Agency
1530 North Main Street
Wheaton, IL 60187
312-653-6400

St. Mary's Services
5725 North Kenmore Avenue
Chicago, IL 60660
312-561-5288

INDIANA

Department of Public Welfare
Child Welfare and Social Services Division
141 South Meridian Street
Indianapolis, IN 46225
317-232-4434

Bethany Christian Services
9595 North Whitley Drive, Suite 210
Indianapolis, IN 46240-1308
317-848-9518

Bethany Christian Services
7895 Broadway, Suite J-1
Merrillville, IN 46410-5529
219-769-0211

Childplace
2420 Highway 62
Jeffersonville, IN 47130
812-282-8240

IOWA

Iowa Department of Human Services
Hoover State Office Building
Des Moines, IA 50319
515-281-5358

Bethany Christian Services
322 Central Avenue N.W.
P.O. Box 143
Orange City, IA 51401-1341
712-737-4831

Bethany Christian Services Community Center
712 Union Street, Room 303
Pella, IA 50219-1768
515-628-4606

KANSAS

State Department of Social & Rehabilitation Services
2700 West 6th Street
Topeka, KS 66606
913-296-4661

Gentle Shepherd Child Placement Services
304 South Clairborne, Suite 201
Olathe, KS 66062
913-764-3811

KENTUCKY

Department of Social Services
275 East Main Street
Frankfort, KY 40621
502-564-2136

Childplace
6105 Outer Loop
Louisville, KY 40219
502-969-0977

LOUISIANA

Louisiana Department of Health & Human Resources
Division of Children, Youth, and Family Services
P.O. Box 3318
Baton Rouge, LA 70821
504-342-4040

Children's Bureau of New Orleans
The Maison Blanche Building
921 Canal Street, Suite 840
New Orleans, LA 70112
504-525-2366

Volunteers of America
354 Jordan Street
Shreveport, LA 71101
318-221-2669

MAINE

Department of Human Services
221 State Street
Augusta, ME 04333
207-289-2972

St. Andre Home, Inc.
283 Elm Street
Biddeford, ME 04005
207-282-3351

MARYLAND

Adoptive Resource Exchange
Social Services Administration
300 West Preston Street
Baltimore, MD 21201
301-576-5313

Bethany Christian Services
114-B Annapolis Street
Annapolis, MD 21401
301-263-7703

MASSACHUSETTS

Department of Social Services
150 Causeway Street
Boston, MA 02114
617-727-0900

Bethany Christian Services
62 Foundry Street
Wakefield, MA 01880-3205
617-246-1890

Our Lady of Providence Children's Center
2112 Riverdale Street
West Springfield, MA 01089
413-788-7366

Catholic Charities of Worcester
15 Ripley Street
Worcester, MA 01610
617-798-0191

Roxbury Children's Services
22 Elm Hill Avenue
Dorchester, MA 02121
617-445-6655

MICHIGAN

Michigan Department of Social Services
P.O. Box 30037
Lansing, MI 48909
517-373-3513

Bethany Christian Services
901 Eastern Avenue N.E.
Grand Rapids, MI 49503-1295
616-459-6273

Bethany Christian Services
6995 West 48th
P.O. Box 173
Fremont, MI 49412-9506
616-924-3390

Bethany Christian Services
Dolly Madison Office Center, Suite 250
32500 Concord Drive
Madison Heights, MI 48071-1140
313-588-9400

Bethany Christian Services
135 North State Street
Zeeland, MI 49464-1212
616-772-9195

Christian Family Services
17105 West 12 Mile Road
Southfield, MI 48076
313-557-8390

MINNESOTA

Minnesota Department of Human Services
Centennial Office Building
St. Paul, MN 55155
612-296-3740

Bethany Christian Services
421 South Main
Stillwater, MN 55082-5127
612-439-9603

New Life Home & Family Services
3361 Republic Avenue Street
Louis Park, MN 55426
612-920-8117

MISSISSIPPI

State Department of Public Welfare
P.O. Box 352
Jackson, MS 39205
601-354-0341

Bethany Christian Services
Woodland Hills Office Building, Suite 545
3000 Old Canton Road
Jackson, MS 39216-4212
601-366-4282

MISSOURI

Department of Social Services
P.O. Box 88
Jefferson City, MO 65103
314-751-2981

The Adams Center
9200 Ward Parkway
Kansas City, MO 64114
816-444-4545

Bethany Christian Services
7750 Clayton Road
St. Louis, MO 63117
314-644-3535

Love Basket
8965 Old LeMay Ferry Road
Hillsboro, MO 63050
314-789-4100

Highlands Child Placement Services
P.O. Box 5040
Kansas City, MO 64129
816-924-6565

MONTANA

Community Services
P.O Box 4210
Helena, MT 59604
406-444-3865

NEBRASKA

Department of Social Services
P.O. Box 95026
Lincoln, NE 68509
402-471-3121

Nebraska Children's Home Society
3549 Fontenelle Blvd.
Omaha, NE 68104
402-451-0787

NEVADA

Department of Human Resources
Nevada State Welfare Division
2527 North Carson Street
Carson City, NV 89701
702-885-3023

NEW HAMPSHIRE

New Hampshire Division for Children & Youth Services
Hazen Drive
Concord, NH 03301
603-271-3602

NEW JERSEY

New Jersey Division of Youth & Family Service
1 South Montgomery Street, C.N. 717
Trenton, NJ 08625
609-633-6991

Bethany Christian Services
475 High Mt. Road
North Haledon, NJ 07508-2603
201-427-2566

NEW MEXICO

New Mexico Department of Human Services
P.O. Box 2348
Santa Fe, NM 87504-2348
505-827-4109

Family & Children's Services, Inc.
Chaparral Program
4401 Lomas, N.E.
Albuquerque, NM 87110
505-243-2551

Christian Placement Services
West Star Route, Box 38
Portales, NM 88130
505-356-4232

NEW YORK

New York State Department of Social Services
40 North Pearl Street
Albany, NY 12243
518-473-2868

Spence-Chapin Services
6 East 94th Street
New York, NY 10028
212-369-0300

Family Services of Westchester
470 Mamaroneck Avenue
White Plains, NY 10605
914-948-8004

Community Maternity Services
27 North Main Avenue
Albany, NY 12203
518-482-8836

Nazareth Life Center
Box 242
Garrison, NY 10524
914-424-3116

NORTH CAROLINA

Department of Human Resources/Division of Social Services
325 North Salisbury Street
Raleigh, NC 27611
919-733-3801

Bethany Christian Services
25 Reed Street, P.O. Box 15569
Asheville, NC 28813-0436
704-272-7146

NORTH DAKOTA

Department of Human Services
State Capital Building
Bismark, ND 58505
701-224-2316

OHIO

Department of Human Services
30 East Broad Street
Columbus, OH 43266
614-466-8510

Bair Foundation
3645 State Route 5
P.O. Box 95
Cortland, OH 44410
216-638-5694

Bethany Christian Services
Walter L. Mitchell Building, Suite 340
1655 West Market Street
Akron, OH 44313-7004
216-867-2362

Gentle Care Adoption Service
48 West Whittier Street
Columbus, OH 43206
614-443-2229

OKLAHOMA

Department of Human Services
P.O. Box 25352
Oklahoma City, OK 73125
405-521-4373

Deaconess Hospital and Home
5501 North Portland
Oklahoma City, OK 73112
405-946-5581

OREGON

Children's Services Division
198 Commercial Street S.E.
Salem, OR 97310
503-378-4452

PLAN (Plan Loving Adoptions Now)
P.O. Box 667
McMinnville, OR 97128
503-472-8452

Adventist Adoption & Family Services National Headquarters
6040 Southeast Belmont Street
Portland, OR 97215
503-232-1211

PENNSYLVANIA

Pennsylvania Adoption Exchange
Box 2675
Harrisburg, PA 17105-2675
717-257-7015

Bair Foundation
241 High Street
New Wilmington, PA 16142
412-946-2220

Bethany Christian Services
The Village Plaza
224 Manor Avenue, P.O. Box 317
Millersville, PA 17551-0417
717-872-0945

Bethany Christian Services
694 Lincoln Avenue
Pittsburgh, PA 15202
412-734-2662

Bethany Christian Services
1107 Bethlehem Pike
Flourtown, PA 19031-1919
215-233-4626

Children's Home of Pittsburgh
5618 Kentucky Avenue
Pittsburgh, PA 15232
412-441-4884

Family Health Council
1200 Allegheny Tower
625 Stanwix Street
Pittsburgh, PA 15222
412-288-2130

Golden Cradle Home
555 East City Line Avenue
Bala Cynwyd, PA 19004
215-289-2229

RHODE ISLAND

Department of Children & Their Families
610 Mt. Pleasant Avenue
Providence, RI 02908
401-457-4545

SOUTH CAROLINA

Department of Social Services
P.O. Box 1520
Columbia, SC 29202
803-734-6112

Tender Loving Care Adoptions Agency
P.O. Box 1094
Fort Mill, SC 29715
803-548-5100

Bethany Christian Services
300 University Ridge, Suite 114
Greenville, SC 29601-3645
803-235-2273

SOUTH DAKOTA

Child Protection Services
Department of Social Services
700 Governors Drive
Pierre, S.D. 57501
605-773-3227

TENNESSEE

Department of Human Services
Citizens Plaza Building
400 Deaderick Street
Nashville, TN 37219
615-741-5935

Bethany Christian Services
4719 Brainerd Road, Suite D
Chattanooga, TN 37411-3830
615-622-7360

Bethany Christian Services
3387 Poplar, Suite 101
Memphis, TN 38111
904-454-1401

TEXAS

Department of Human Services
P.O. Box 2960
Austin, TX 78769
512-450-3357

Texas Cradle Society
8222 Wurzbach
San Antonio, TX 78229
512-696-7700

The Edna Gladney Home
2300 Hemphill Street
Fort Worth, TX 76110
817-926-3304

Southwest Maternity Center
6487 Whitby Road
San Antonio, TX 78240
512-696-2410

Homes of St. Mark
1302 Marshall
Houston, TX 77006
713-522-2800

Children Service Bureau
625 North Alamo
San Antonio, TX 78215
512-223-6281

Smithlawn Home & Adoption Agency
Box 6451
Lubbock, TX 79413
806-745-2574

UTAH

Division of Family Services
150 West North Temple Street
Salt Lake City, UT 84103
801-533-7123

VERMONT

Vermont Social Services
103 S. Main Street
Waterbury, VT 05676
802-241-2150

VIRGINIA

Department of Social Services
8007 Discovery Drive
Richmond, VA 23228
804-281-9131

Bethany Christian Services
246 Maple Avenue
East Vienna, VA 22180-4631
703-255-4775

WASHINGTON

Division of Children & Family Services
OB41-C
Olympia, WA 98504
206-753-0965

Burden Bearers
424 North 139th
Seattle, WA 98133
206-367-4600

Bethany Christian Services
103 East Holly, Suite 316
Bellingham, WA 98225-4718
206-733-6042

New Hope of Washington
11000 Lake City Way N.E., Suite 400
Seattle, WA 98125
206-363-1800

WEST VIRGINIA

Department of Human Services
1900 Washington Street E.
Charleston, WV 25305
304-348-7980

WISCONSIN

Department of Health & Social Service
P.O. Box 7851
Madison, WI 53707
608-266-0690

Bethany Christian Services
W255 N477 Grandview Blvd., Suite 207
Waukesha, WI 53188-1606
414-547-6557

WYOMING

Division of Public Assistance and Social Services
Hathaway Building
Cheyenne, WY 82002-0710
307-777-6891

Agencies Specializing in Foreign Adoptions

ASIA (Adoption Services Information Agency)
7720 Alaska Avenue N.W.
Washington, D.C. 20012
202-726-7193

Adoption Advocates International
658 Black Diamond Road
Port Angeles, WA 98362
206-452-4777

American Adoption Agency
1228 M Street N.W.
Washington, D.C. 20005
202-638-1543

Americans for International Aid and Adoption
877 South Adams
Birmingham, MI 48011
313-645-2211

Associated Catholic Charities
1231 Prytania Street
New Orleans, LA 70130
504-523-3755

Bethany Christian Services
901 Eastern Avenue N.E.
Grand Rapids, MI 49503
616-459-6273 or 800-BETHANY

Children's Home Society of Minnesota
2230 Como Avenue
St. Paul, MN 55108
612-646-6393

Children's Services International
1819 Peachtree Road N.E., Suite 318
Atlanta, GA 30309-1847
404-355-3233

Covenant Children
P.O. Box 341490
Memphis, TN 38184-1490
901-528-5854

Friends of Children of Various Nations
600 Gilpin Street
Denver, CO 80218
303-321-8251

Globe International Adoptions
6330 West Villa Theresa Drive
Glendale, AZ 85308
602-843-7276

Holt International Children's Services
P.O. Box 2880
Eugene, OR 98402
503-687-2202

House of Samuel
11777 South Old Nogales Highway
Tucson, AZ 85706
602-294-1997

International Adoptions
282 Moody Street
Waltham, MA 02154
617-894-5330

International Christian Adoption Agency
60 West River Road
Waterville, ME 04901
207-872-2156

International Social Services/American Branch
95 Madison Avenue
New York, NY 10016
212-532-5858

Love Basket
8965 Old LeMay Ferry Road
Hillsboro, MO 63050
314-789-4100

Love the Children
221 West Broad Street
Quakertown, PA 18951
215-536-4180

Open Arms
16429 Northeast 133rd Court
Redmond, WA 98052
206-881-7475

Plan Adoption Services
P.O. Box 667
McMinnville, OR 97128
503-472-8452

Universal Aid for Children
8760 Northeast Second Avenue
Miami Shores, FL 33138
305-754-4886

Welcome House
P.O. Box 836
Doylestown, PA 18901
215-345-0430

Agencies Specializing in Hard to Place Children

AASK America (Aid to Adoption of Special Kids)
1540 Market Street
San Francisco, CA 94102
415-626-5527

The CAP Book
700 Exchange Street
Rochester, New York 14608
716-232-5110
(Provides a national registry of hard to place children.)

Children Unlimited
P.O. Box 11463
Columbia, SC 29211
803-799-8311

Children's Adoption Resource Exchange
1039 Evarts Street N.E.
Washington, D.C. 20017
202-526-5200

Family Builders by Adoption
1515 Webster Street
Oakland, CA 94612
415-272-0204

Family Services Center
Project CAN
2960 Roosevelt Boulevard
Clearwater, FL 33520
813-531-0481

Lutheran Child and Family Services
7620 Madison Street
River Forest, IL 60305
312-771-7180

Medina Children's Service
P.O. Box 22638
Seattle, WA 98122
206-324-9470

National Resource Center for
Special Needs Adoption
Spaulding for Children
3660 Waltrous Road
Chelsea, MI 48118
313-475-8693

North American Council on Adoptable Children
P.O. Box 14808
Minneapolis, MN 55414
612-333-7692

Project IMPACT
25 West Street
Boston, MA 02111
617-451-1472

Tressler-Lutheran Service Associates
25 West Springettsburg Avenue
York, PA 17403
717-845-9113

Women's Christian Alliance
1610-14 North Broad Street
Philadelphia, PA 19121
215-236-9911

Suggested Reading

Helpful Reading on Infertility

American Fertility Society. Supplies information on qualified specialists and publishes material on infertility. 2140 Eleventh Avenue South, Suite 200, Birmingham, Alabama 35205; 205-933-8494.

Barker, Graham, M.D. *Search For Fertility.* (New York: William Morrow and Company, 1980).

DeJong, Peter, and Smit, William. *Planning Your Family: How to Decide What's Best for You.* (Grand Rapids, Michigan: Zondervan Publishing House, 1987).

Hanes, Mari with Hayford, Jack. *Beyond Heartache.* (Wheaton, Illinois: Living Books, Tyndale House Publishers, 1984).

Lifchez, Aaron S., M.D., and Fenton, Judith A. *The Fertility Handbook.* (New York: Clarkson N. Potter, 1980).

Love, Vicky. *Childless Is Not Less.* (Minneapolis, Minnesota: Bethany House Publishers, 1984).

Resolve. Newsletter for infertile couples. 5 Water Street, Arlington, Maine 02174; 617-643-2424.

Silber, Sherman J., M.D. *How To Get Pregnant*. (New York: Charles Scribner and Sons, 1980).

Stepping Stones. Newsletter for infertile couples. Box 11141, Wichita, Kansas 67211.

Stigger, Judith. *Coping With Infertility: A Guide for Couples, Families, and Counselors*. (Minneapolis, Minnesota: Augsburg Publishing House, 1983).

Stout, Martha. *Without Child*. (Grand Rapids, Michigan: Zondervan Publishing House, 1985).

Van Regenmorter, John and Sylvia, and McIlhaney, Joe S., M.D. *Dear God, Why Can't We Have A Baby?* (Grand Rapids, Michigan: Baker Book House, 1986).

Helpful Reading on Adoption

Adopted Child: A Newsletter for Parents. Published monthly by Lois R. Melina, P.O. Box 9362, Moscow, Idaho 83843.

Adoption Factbook: United States Data, Issues, Regulations and Resources. National Committee for Adoption, 2025 M. Street, N.W. Suite 512, Washington, D.C. 20036, 1985.

Blank, J. P. *Nineteen Steps Up the Mountain: The Story of the DeBolt Family*. (New York: Lippincott, 1976).

Booth, Nyla and Scott, Ann. *Room For One More*. (Wheaton, Illinois: Tyndale House, 1984).

Carney, Ann. *No More Here and There*. (Chapel Hill, N.C.: University of North Carolina Press, 1976).

Family Building Through Adoption. Course booklet on adoption published by FACE (Families Adopting Children Everywhere), Box 28058, Northwood Station, Baltimore, Maryland 21239; 301-256-0410.

Felker, Donald W., and Felker, Evelyn H. *Adoption: Beginning to End—A Guide for Christian Parents*. (Grand Rapids, Michigan: Baker Book House, 1987).

Gilman, Lois. *The Adoption Resource Book*. (New York: Harper & Row, 1984, 1987).

Jewett, Claudia. *Adopting The Older Child*. (Boston, Massachussetts: Harvard Common Press, 1978).

Kiemel-Anderson, Ann. *And With the Gift Came Laughter*. (Wheaton, Illinois: Tyndale House, 1987).

Kravik, Patricia J. *Adopting Children With Special Needs*. (New York: North American Council on Adoptable Children, 1976).

Lasnick, Roberts. *A Parents's Guide To Adoption*. (New York: Sterling Publishing Co., 1979).

Lifton, B. J. *Twice Born: Memoirs Of An Adopted Daughter*. (New York: McGraw Hill, 1975).

Macmanus, Sheila. *The Adoption Book.* (Mahwah, New Jersey: Paulist Press, 1984).

Martin, Cynthia D. *Beating the Adoption Game.* (San Diego, California: Oaktree Publications, 1980).

Ross, Bette. *Our Special Child.* (Old Tappan, New Jersey: Fleming H. Revell, 1984).

Sorosky, Arthur D., M.D., Baron, Annette, M.S.W., and Pannor, Reuben, M.S.W. *The Adoption Triangle: Sealed or Open Records: How They Affect Adoptees, Birth Parents, and Adoptive Parents,* revised edition. (New York: Anchor Press/Doubleday, 1984).

Strom, Kay Marshall. *Chosen Families.* (Grand Rapids, Michigan: Zondervan Publishing House, 1985).

Valenti, Laura. *The Fifteen Most Asked Questions About Adoption.* (Scottdale, Pennsylvania: Herald Press, 1985).

Waybill, Marjorie. *Chinese Eyes.* (Scottdale, Pennsylvania: Herald Press, 1974). (also for children)

Helpful Reading on Miscarriage

Borg, Susan, and Lasker, Judith. *When Pregnancy Fails: Families Coping With Miscarriage, Stillbirth, and Infant Death.* (Boston, Massachussetts: Beacon Press, 1981).

Friedman, Rochelle, and Gradstein, Bonnie. *Surviving Pregnancy Loss.* (Boston, Massachussetts and New York: Little, Brown, 1982).

Kiemel Anderson, Ann. *Taste of Tears, Touch of God.* (Nashville, Tennessee: Thomas Nelson, 1984).

Vredevelt, Pam. *Empty Arms.* (Portland, Oregon: Multnomah Press, 1984).

Helpful Reading on Suffering

Landorf, Joyce. *The High Cost of Growing.* (New York: Bantam Books, 1979).

Lewis, C.S. *A Grief Observed.* (New York: Walker and Company, 1985).

Schaeffer, Edith. *Affliction.* (Old Tappan, New Jersey: Fleming H. Revell, 1979).

Yancey, Philip. *Where Is God When It Hurts?* (Grand Rapids, Michigan: Zondervan Publishing House, 1984).